Decorating Cakes for
SPECIAL OCCASIONS

by the same author
HOME-MADE, AND AT A FRACTION OF THE COST
DECORATING CAKES FOR CHILDREN'S PARTIES

Decorating Cakes for
SPECIAL OCCASIONS
POLLY PINDER

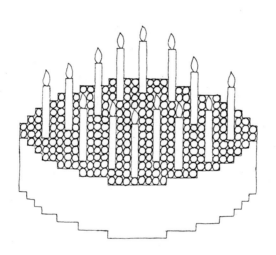

SEARCH PRESS

First published 1985

by Search Press Ltd.,
Wellwood, North Farm Road,
Tunbridge Wells, Kent TN2 3DR

ISBN (UK) 0 85532 562 3

Printed in Spain by Elkar S. Coop, Bilbao-12

Contents

Introduction

Ever since I began work on my first cake book *Decorating Cakes for Children's Parties*, designing cakes has become a kind of marvellous obsession. Luckily the possibilities seem limitless, as do effective and amusing subjects; for I hope that this new book will also bring a touch of humour to the cake decorating scene in general.

Readers of the first book will know that my previous experience of cake decorating was nil; and I still, whenever I gaze in wonder at the intricate designs of the traditionally iced cake, consider myself a novice. I learned a great deal, however, while working on the first book, and now my knowledge has been extended still further – not least by the delight of discovering that I can actually pipe a 'real' flower (page 33) and create a piece of lattice work (page 38). I hope that this will encourage anyone who considers cake decorating to be beyond their present skill – all that is required for success is planning, time, and patience.

Patience is certainly needed when one is trying to make pieces of cake fit properly into the design and on to each other, or when, for instance, balancing the arch above the door of the house-warming cake. Perhaps my greatest 'fiddle' came in reproducing the individual silken tassels on the graduation cake. In addition, I hope that some of the techniques I have adopted will work as a springboard for readers who are trying out new ideas. Although I am sure it must have been done before, I have never seen the sort of marquetry, or 'marbling', I have attempted in the Easter cake.

Some readers of my first book have mentioned that I gave no directions for 'cutting' the cakes. I realise, of course, that this is a particularly important part of most celebratory parties, but I can only suggest that the cake be dismantled, as far as possible, and then cut in the way which seems most obvious to the cutter; I feel one should not be too precise about it – some of the designs are so complex (compared to the conventional square or round decorated cakes) that it is too much to expect to end up with a perfectly neat little square for each person. My feeling is, the time and patience taken in completing the cake are fully rewarded by the reaction of onlookers – the moment of presentation, the shouts of acclamation and recognition that ring out (it really does happen, particularly if a little alcohol has previously been consumed!). That will fill the decorator with enough pride to last at least until the next cake! – and the fact that one can eat the cake, in whatever shape, is a bonus.

General Notes

The cakes

As the mixture for these cakes is the traditional rich fruit, they can be made weeks, or even months, in advance. Although many people prefer to use their own favourite recipe for this type of cake, I have drawn up a chart on page 127 with ingredients and quantities for the particular size and shape required. For those with preference for a sponge mixture, there is a separate chart, on the same page, giving similar details.

Method for baking rich fruit cake

Line the cake tin with a double thickness of greased (melted lard or oil) greaseproof paper and tie a double thickness of brown paper round the outside.

Pre-heat the oven to 300°F (150°C), Gas Mark 2.

Most of the dried fruit bought now is pre-washed, but it may be as well to sort through for any pieces of stalk or grit.

Quarter the cherries and, if necessary, chop the mixed peel. Wash in warm water and dry thoroughly.

Put the currants, raisins, sultanas, cherries, mixed peel, grated lemon rind and almonds in a basin. Mix thoroughly. Sieve the flour, cinnamon and spice into another basin. Mix thoroughly. Cream the butter in another basin, then add the sugar. Cream until light and fluffy. Beat in the black treacle. Add the eggs, one at a time. Beat well and add a tablespoon (tblsp) of flour mixture after each egg. Carefully fold in the remaining flour, then fold in the fruit. Stir in most of the brandy (keep 1-2 tablespoons to be added after baking.)

Transfer the mixture to the tin. Using a wet spoon, spread it evenly, making a slight hollow in the centre.

Place the tin on folded newspaper in the centre of the oven. For the larger cakes, reduce heat to 275°F (140°C), Gas Mark 1, after two-thirds of the baking time.

To test whether baking is complete, insert a skewer into the centre of the cake: it should come out clean.

When the cake is completely cold, wrap it in greaseproof paper and place in an air-tight tin – if the cake is too large for a tin, wrap it securely in tin foil.

After one week remove the cake from its wrapping, pierce the top, at intervals, with a skewer and carefully pour in the remaining brandy. Re-wrap and keep for four to five more weeks.

Marzipan

To make 450g (1lb) of marzipan, mix in a basin 110g (4oz) of caster sugar, 110g (4oz) icing sugar and 220g (8oz) of ground almonds. Make a well in the centre and add 1 teaspoon (teasp) of lemon juice, $\frac{1}{2}$ teaspoon of orange flower water and a few drops of almond essence (a teaspoon of rum can be added if the cake is to be kept for months rather than weeks.) Mix thoroughly, then add sufficient beaten egg to make a manageable paste. Turn on to a dusted (50/50 mixture of icing sugar and cornflour) surface and knead gently until smooth. Wrap securely in cling film until required.

When you are ready to decorate, the cake should be brushed with warm sieved apricot jam, then covered with the marzipan. The cake must then be left to dry for 48 hours.

Fondant

This is an icing which has liquid glucose added to make it pliable and easy to model. To make 450g (1lb) drop the white of an egg in to a basin and slowly mix in 450g (1lb) of sieved icing sugar and 2 tablespoons of warmed liquid glucose. The quantities of icing sugar and egg white are not absolutely critical, more or less of one or the other may be needed to achieve the correct consistency, which should be easy and firm to work with – if it feels floppy, add some more sieved icing sugar; if it becomes stiff and difficult to handle, add a little more egg white. Some recipes require one quarter of an egg white. As this is difficult to measure, make a rough guess, being generous rather than careful.

Egg white is also needed to secure pieces of fondant to vertical parts of the cake. This should be applied sparingly

with a pastry brush or small paint brush – if too much is used, the fondant will slip off or begin to weep at the seams.

Fondant which is not needed immediately should be wrapped in cling film and kept in an air-tight box at room temperature, not in the refrigerator.

Ready-made commercial fondant can be bought in 220g ($\frac{1}{2}$lb) blocks from cake-decorating specialists and some supermarkets. It is very convenient if you are short of time.

Flavour and colour is added to the fondant at the kneading stage, when all the icing sugar and glucose have been mixed in. If pale fondant is required add the colour, drop by drop, from a metal skewer. When a large piece of fondant needs to have a very deep colour, make a well in the centre, carefully pour in the colour, then give a liberal shake with the dredger (containing 50% icing sugar and 50% cornflour) and knead thoroughly.

Gum tragacanth (powdered gum) is sometimes used as a hardening agent. Use 1-2 teaspoonsful per 220g (8oz) of icing sugar. It is very useful if the fondant is to remain flat, but problems start when you mould and shape round cakes, for it dries rapidly and fine cracks can appear on the surface. The secret is to work quickly. The gum can be bought from most chemists. It is rather expensive but worth having if you intend to do more than one fondant cake.

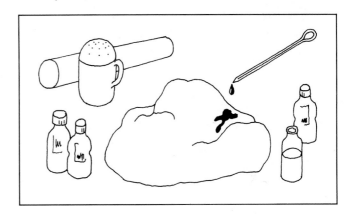

Royal icing and piped writing

To make 220g (8oz) of royal icing, drop one egg white into a very clean basin (with no trace of grease) and slowly mix in 220g (8oz) of sieved icing sugar. This can be done by hand or in the mixer, using a beater rather than a whisk, on the slowest speed.

Again, the quantities are not critical: you may need more or less of one or the other to obtain the correct consistency. Some recipes need only one-eighth of an egg white. As with the fondant, make a rough guess, erring on the side of generosity. The correct consistency can really only be judged after a little practice with the icing bag – it should be neither too runny to lose its shape, nor too stiff to flow easily from the bag.

As with the fondant, add colour, drop by drop, from a metal skewer. To obtain a shaded effect of piped work, drop a generous teaspoonful each of two coloured icings, side by side, into the bag.

If you have not done piped writing before, it may be as well to practise on the table top first.

To pipe directly on to the iced cake, first write the word on greaseproof paper, then attach the paper, with two dabs of royal icing, to the cake. Stick a sewing needle, at intervals, through the pencil lines. Remove the paper. Use the needle marks as guides and the original drawn letters as reference.

To centre a word on the cake, using a tape measure or ruler, find the centre of the cake and mark with a pin. Find the centre of the word by measuring, mark with a pencil, then lay the pencil mark over the pin mark.

Royal icing can be stored in an airtight container and kept in the refrigerator for as long as three weeks, after which it will have to be gently beaten again before being used.

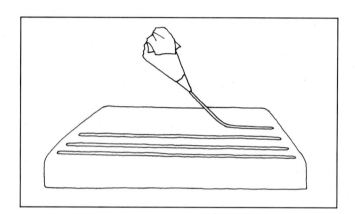

Spacers

Spacers are used to ensure an even piece of flat fondant or marzipan. They are placed at each side so that the rolling pin rolls over them and the fondant/marzipan at the same time.

Spacers can be bought from cake-decorating specialists but it is cheaper to buy a packet of flat lolly sticks (LS) and make your own. These are usually about 2mm (1/10in.) thick. Make four spacers (use cellotape to join the lolly sticks together) 4 LS long, the first pair 1 LS thick and the second pair 2 LS thick – see the drawing. Sometimes a piece of fondant needs to be 3 or 4 LS thick. As these pieces are usually quite small the spacers do not have to be long – simply cellotape the required number together. Again, see the illustration.

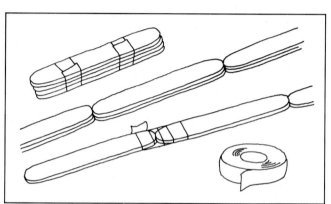

Icing bags and nozzles

I prefer to make my own disposable bags. They are more convenient and easier to use than the commercial tubes and bags, which one has to be continually washing when using different coloured icings.

Buy a packet of flat sheets of greaseproof paper (rather than a roll). Cut a strip off the sheet to make a square. See the illustration: fold the square into a triangle; fold point **A** to point **C**; then point **B** to point **D**; then point **C** to point **E**. Snip a small piece from point **X**. Open the bag, drop the nozzle in, making sure that half of it comes out at the bottom. Drop in a couple of teaspoons of royal icing, fold the flap over, fold the two corners **Y** and **Z** inwards, then pipe away! As the icing is used, fold the top of the bag over again.

Ateco icing nozzles have been used for most of the pipe work on the cakes in this book, but if they are not available in your area you can use the equivalent in another make – where possible I have drawn the nozzles and the shape produced by each.

You can buy a small nozzle brush – which is extremely useful when washing the nozzles – from cake-decorating specialists or kitchen equipment shops.

Apricot jam

This is used to coat the cakes before applying marzipan (apricot has the least intrusive flavour). It should be gently heated with a little water and then sieved to remove skin and hard pieces, just prior to brushing a thin film on to the cakes.

Colouring

The basic colours can be bought from most supermarkets. For unusual shades you will probably have to go to a cake-decorating specialist. The only *edible* gold and silver I have found comes in powdered form.

Steel rule

This can be bought from cake-decorating specialists and some kitchen equipment shops. It is used to ensure a perfectly flat surface when covering a cake with royal icing – I use it as a straight edge for cutting fondant and marzipan.

Hints

A flexible tape measure, rather than a ruler, is handy for measuring the cake, marzipan and fondant pieces.

When measuring a cake which has to be cut in to a complex shape, use coloured-headed pins as markers, just pushing them half in to the cake.

A turn-table is extremely useful when decorating the cakes. I find the home-made version (placing the cake board on a plate and then on top of an inverted plate) not really adequate – but it could suffice.

Sponge cake mixture

This can be used as an alternative to the rich fruit mixture. A chart with ingredients and quantities for the size and shape of the cake required, is given on page 127.

This is the method for baking: beat the butter and sugar until pale and fluffy (substitute margarine for butter if desired). Gradually add alternate equal quantities of flour, ground rice and beaten egg and milk. The mixture should have a soft dropping consistency, a little more milk may be needed. The cakes are baked in the centre of the oven at 350°F (180°C), Gas Mark 4, and are ready when a firm, light-golden crust has formed and the cake has come slightly away from the sides of the tin. Allow to cool in the tin before removing, then leave overnight on a wire tray.

The plain sponge mixture can be varied in several ways: by adding glacé cherries, chopped walnuts, raisins, chopped bananas or honey (as a rough guide, if the recipe requires 220g (8oz) of butter, add the same quantity of fruit or nuts); by substituting one tablespoon (tblsp) of flour and one of ground rice for two tablespoons of cocoa powder; or by adding essences, orange, lemon, raspberry, etc. The larger cakes can be split and filled with butter cream and/or jam. (If a cake has to be cut into different shapes, it is better to add a flavouring rather than fruit or nuts.)

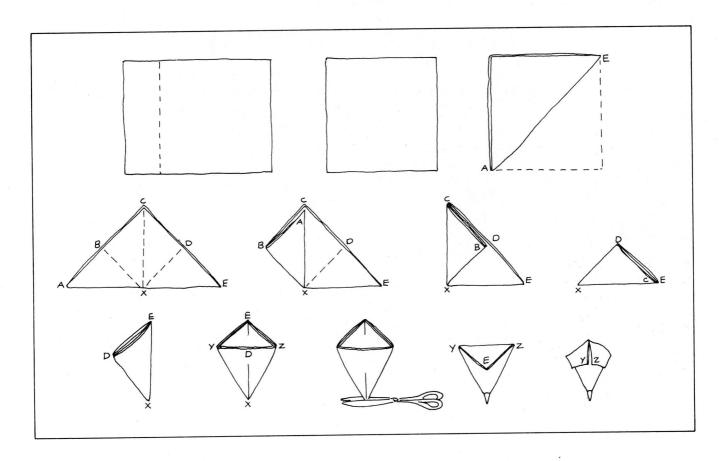

Special Occasions

Twenty-first birthday

Although eighteen is now usually considered the age of majority, twenty-one will, I believe, always be an important birthday. The figures on the cake depict four stages: one-year-old potty training; the over-energetic, ever dirty seven-year-old; the 'try anything and everything' fourteen-year-old – if this bears no resemblance at all to your own child, you could remove the (illegal) beer and cigarette, but keep the spots; and the grown-up, confident, very sensible twenty-one-year-old.

This cake is obviously for a boy, but the figures can easily be changed. Directions are given in caption 19.

The structure is made from a 300mm (12in.) square cake. Ingredients and quantities for this are given on page 127 and method for baking on page 6–7. Instructions for making royal icing, marzipan and fondant are on page 7. If you are making your own fondant, you will find it easier to make the 2kg (4½lb) in four batches, keeping each piece securely wrapped in cling film and in an airtight container until required.

The cake will take one to two days to decorate, after the covering of marzipan has been left to dry for 48 hours.

Please read the General Notes on pages 6 to 9 before starting to decorate. Also read through the step-by-step instructions and check the ingredient and equipment lists.

Ingredients for fondant and royal icing

2kg (4½lb) icing sugar, plus 170g (6oz)
4½ egg whites, plus ¾
9 tblsp liquid glucose
flavouring (optional)
Also: 1.340kg (3lb) marzipan; warm sieved apricot jam; 50/50 mixture of icing sugar and cornflour in a dusting dredger; yellow, red, flesh, blue, black, brown and gold food colouring.

Equipment

Mixing bowls; spoons; sieve; rolling pin; steel rule; sharp-pointed knife; lolly sticks (LS) as spacers; pastry brush; small paint brush; greaseproof paper; Ateco (or equivalent) icing nozzles 1, 2 and 4; 50mm (2in.) round cutter; coloured-headed sewing pins; 21 candles and candle holders; sewing needle; 30mm (12in.) square silver cake board.

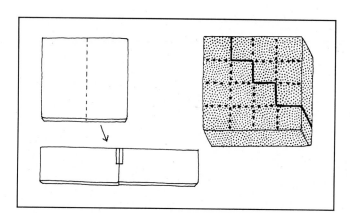

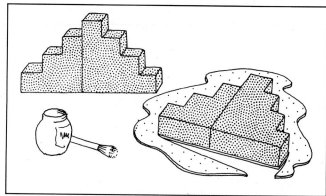

1. Cut the cake board in half using a serrated bread knife or saw. Put the two pieces together and stick a piece of cellotape over the join, underneath and halfway across the top.

Slice the top of the cake flat, then mark, with the pins, into sixteen 75mm (3in.) squares. Cut carefully.

2. Join the cake together with jam and a slice of marzipan 1 LS thick. Brush back of cake with jam. Roll marzipan to 1 LS thick, lay cake on top and cut around the shape. Carefully lift and repeat with front, then each step, using marzipan at 2 LS thick.

Leave to dry for 48 hours.

3. Brush the back of the cake with a thin film of egg white. Roll 670g (1½lb) of white fondant (upon a generously dusted surface) to 1 LS thick and roughly to the shape of the cake. Lay cake on fondant and cut round.

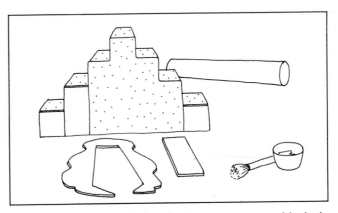

4. Take 110g (4oz) of white fondant trimmings, add a little yellow, and roll to 2 LS thick. Cover the outer squares, securing with egg white. Add remaining white trimmings to yellow trimmings and add more yellow colouring. Roll to 2 LS thick and cover next two panels as shown.

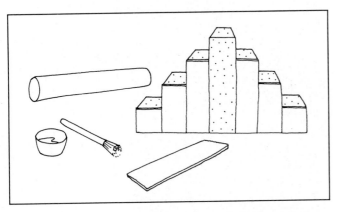

5. Add 220g (8oz) of fondant to trimmings and more yellow colouring. Cover the next two panels. Add 170g (6oz) fondant to trimmings, add yellow and drops of red to make bright orange, then cover centre panel.

6. Take 450g (1lb) of white fondant. Measure each step in turn, roll fondant to 2 LS thick, cut to fit, then apply. Start at the bottom of each side, covering top step last. Roll 110g (4oz) of white fondant to 1 LS thick and cut four 50mm (2in.) circles. Leave them to dry on a dusted surface.

7. Make the royal icing.
   Draw four 50mm (2in.) circles on greaseproof paper, then trace 21, 14, 7 and 1 in each. Attach paper circles, with two dabs of icing, to fondant circles, then prick through the pencil lines with the needle. With *No. 2 nozzle* and orange icing, follow the needle marks.

8. Add drops of water to some orange icing and, using a skewer or small spoon, fill in the numbers. Leave to dry for two hours.
   With *No. 2 nozzle* and orange icing, pipe lines of continuous dots on panel seams, then pipe lines of white continuous dots inside the orange ones.

11

The ages depicted here are, I feel, fairly typical and certainly add humour to the theme of the cake; but if the slouching fourteen-year-old seems to be going too far for your own child you can remove the cigarette and beer (not least on legal grounds!) – but keep the spots!

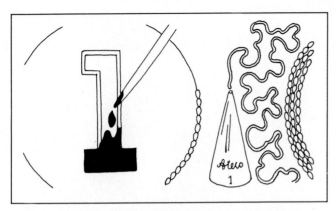

9. Secure the circles to the appropriate panels with egg white. Pipe orange continuous dots around each circle, then two more around '21'. With *nozzle No. 1* and orange icing, pipe squiggly lines all over the centre panel. When dry, paint these and the lines around '21' gold.

10. Carefully lift the cake and secure it to the silver cake board with smears of icing. With *No. 4* and white icing, pipe a line of continuous dots along the front and back of the bottom edge.

Take 110g (4oz) of fondant. Colour 90g (3oz) with flesh and the remainder blue.

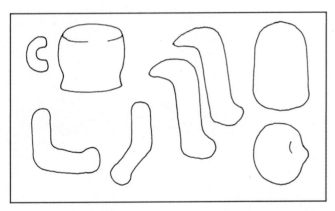

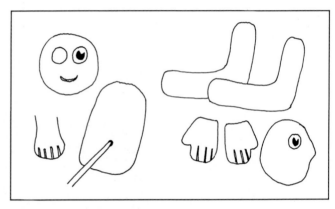

11. Model a handle and potty, as shown. Attach the handle with egg white and support with 2 LS until dry. Secure the potty to the lowest step with a blob of icing. Model the pieces, legs first, and attach with egg white; then the body and arms, as shown. Model the head.

12. Flatten two little white balls, attach as shown. Paint the eyes, then attach the head to the body. Mark fingers, toes and mouth with a knife, tummy button with the paint brush handle.

With about 45g (1½oz) of flesh fondant model legs, hands and head for next figure. Attach and paint eyes.

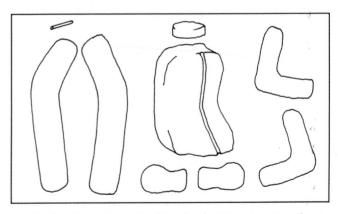

13. Mark a mouth. Model brown trousers and attach to legs. Model and attach brown shoes. Model green body, bend slightly, then attach to trousers and step. Model arms, attach, then secure hands. Paint freckles across nose and dirt (watered-down black) on cheeks and chin. Attach head to body and side of step.

14. Roll a tiny piece of white fondant to cigarette shape, leave to dry. Colour about 60g (2oz) of fondant brown. Model and attach legs for fourteen-year-old. Model black shoes and attach, supporting until secure. Colour about 90g (3oz) of fondant blue. Model and attach body, slouching, and arms.

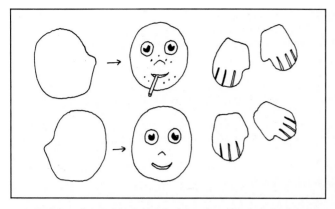

15. Colour about 60g (2oz) of fondant flesh. Model two heads and four hands. Mark fingers and mouths with knife. Attach and paint eyes. Push cigarette carefully into the corner of a mouth, then paint red spots on chin and nose. Attach this head to the blue body.

16. Colour about 60g (2oz) of fondant black. Model and attach legs, as shown. Model and attach dark brown shoes, supporting the left-hand one until secure. Model and attach glass of beer.

17. With about 75g (2½oz) of white fondant, model and attach body, collar and arms. Attach head and hands. Model and attach a black bow-tie.

18. With *No. 1 nozzle* and appropriate coloured icing, pipe the hair: a little for baby; slightly dishevelled for seven-year-old; long and unkempt for fourteen-year-old and fairly neat for 'birthday boy'. Pipe a moustache if appropriate. Insert candle holders and candles – eight on first two steps and five on the third.

19. Figures for a girl: baby remains the same. Model a little skirt, as shown, for next figure. Colour fondant for body and sleeves pale green. I would suggest keeping the cigarette for the fourteen-year-old, children usually try it at about this age, and the spots, but change the large beer glass to a smaller one and pipe longer hair. Model a skirt and legs, as shown. You could paint red lips and green eye shadow to indicate first experiments with make-up. For the last figure, model dress, then legs, then arms in one piece, then neck. Pipe straps and lace on bodice, necklace and bracelet. Paint these and shoes gold.

Graduation

This is not difficult to decorate, but patience is needed for the mortar board tassel – so much colour is required to make the icing a dense black, the tassel strands tends to break while being piped. It is easier to pipe over the broken ones than to try to pick them off. I have chosen black because it is the most common, or used to be. However, if the university or college colours are different, do use them, and change the cushion colour if it is not complementary. I have drawn a basic coat-of-arms shape, but you will have to fill in the appropriate details. A reference can usually be found in the college prospectus.

The mortar board is made from a 200mm (8in.) square cake and the cushion from a 300mm (12in.) square. The ingredients and quantities for these are given on page 127 and method for baking on page 6–7. Instructions for making royal icing, marzipan and fondant are on page 7. If you are making your own fondant, it will be easier to make the 1.570kg (3½lb) in three batches, keeping it securely wrapped in cling film and in an airtight container.

The cake will take one to two days to decorate, after the covering of marzipan has been left to dry for 48 hours.

Please read the General Notes on pages 6 to 9 before starting to decorate. Also read through the step-by-step instructions and check the ingredient and equipment lists.

Ingredients for fondant and royal icing

1.570kg (3½lb) icing sugar, plus 340g (12oz)
3½ egg whites, plus 1½
7 tblsp liquid glucose
flavouring (optional)
Also: 1.340kg (3lb) marzipan; warm sieved apricot jam; 50/50 mixture of cornflour and icing sugar in a dusting dredger; appropriate colours for mortar board, cushion and coat-of-arms, plus silver.

Equipment

Mixing bowls; spoons; sieve; rolling pin; steel rule; sharp-pointed knife; lolly sticks (LS) to use as spacers; pastry brush; small paint brush; greaseproof paper; Ateco (or equivalent) icing nozzles 1, 2 and 3; Bekenal (or similar) icing nozzle 37; 360mm (14in.) square silver cake board; waxed paper; broom handle; cellotape.

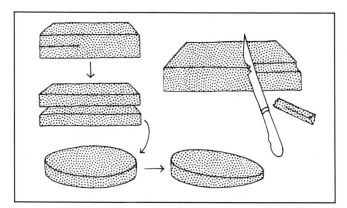

1. Slice the smaller cake in half. Cut a 150mm (6in.) circle from the top half, then slice the top of this so that it slopes, as shown. Cut away the square edges from each of the four sides of the larger cake, as shown, then carefully round off.

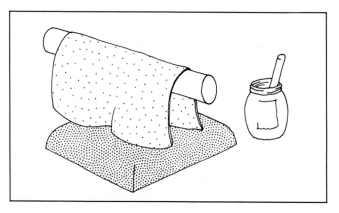

2. Position the large cake on silver board. Roll 900g (2lb) of marzipan to 2 LS thick. Brush cake with jam and, with the help of rolling pin, apply marzipan. Smooth with hands and trim edges.

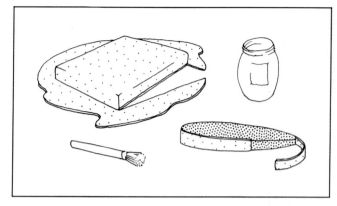

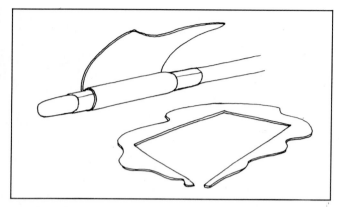

3. Add remaining marzipan to trimmings from cushion. Brush top and sides of smaller square cake with jam, then cover with marzipan 2 LS thick. Apply a piece 1 LS thick to under-side. Cut a strip 2 LS thick and cover sides of round cake.

Leave everything to dry for 48 hours.

4. Meanwhile, take 220g (8oz) of fondant. Wrap a piece of waxed paper round the end of a broom handle, secure with cellotape. Roll fondant to 1 LS thick and cut a rectangle 180mm x 200mm (7in. x 8in.). Carefully wrap this around handle, over waxed paper. Leave to dry until cake is almost complete.

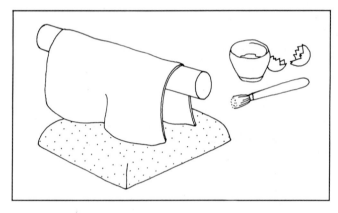

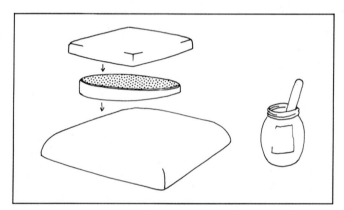

5. Roll white fondant trimmings to 1 LS thick. Cut out shape of university coat-of-arms. Leave to dry.

Take 900g (2lb) of fondant and colour for cushion. Brush sides of cake with egg white, then cover as with marzipan, caption 2. Add 450g (1lb) of fondant to trimmings and colour for mortar board.

6. Cover square and round cakes as with marzipan, caption 3, using egg white instead of jam. Brush top of round cake with jam and attach to underside of square cake. Brush underside of round cake with jam and position on cushion.

Make the 340g (12oz) of royal icing.

7. With *nozzle No. 37* and white icing, pipe braid around cushion. With *No. 3* pipe corner tassels. With *No. 1* pipe appropriate details on coat-of-arms. Using *No. 2 nozzle* and icing a shade lighter than cushion, pipe **Congratulations**, as shown.

Colour icing for the mortar board.

8. With *No. 2* pipe a line of continuous dots around bottom edge, then pipe tassel. Carefully remove degree from broom handle. With *No. 3* pipe ribbon round centre. Paint cushion braid, ribbon and coat-of-arms details with silver. Secure degree and coat-of-arms on cushion with egg white.

Engagement

The Greeks exchanged rings as tokens of love, but it is thought that the Romans developed the custom of prospective husbands giving their brides a ring (anulus pronubis) as a form of warranty. The ring was given at a formal betrothal ceremony where the bride's father also made a solemn pledge of marriage.

This was my second attempt at an engagement cake. The first was a twisting road ending at a rose-clad cottage and symbolising the path of life on which the couple are about to embark. The result was rather obscure, so I decided to change to a simpler idea – the ring.

The cake can be decorated in one to two days. I have not piped names because I felt they would detract from the combination of a simple case and an ornate ring. However, names do personalise a cake so you could use pale blue icing and pipe at either side of the front point of the case: or use dark blue and pipe the names on the heart inside the lid.

The two cakes are baked in two 150mm (6in.) heart-shaped tins – use the recipe for a 150mm (6in.) round cake for each of these. Ingredients and quantities are given on page 127 and the method for baking on page 6–7. Instructions for making royal icing, marzipan and fondant are given on page 7.

Please read the General Notes on pages 6 to 9 before starting to decorate. Also read through the step-by-step instructions and check the ingredient and equipment lists.

Ingredients for fondant and royal icing

800g (1¾lb) icing sugar, plus 60g (2oz)
1¾ egg whites, plus ¼
3½ tblsp liquid glucose
flavouring (optional)
Also: 670g (1½lb) marzipan; warm sieved apricot jam; 50/50 mixture of cornflour and icing sugar in a dusting dredger; blue, red, gold and silver food colouring.

Equipment

Mixing bowls; spoons; sieve; rolling pin; steel rule; sharp-pointed knife; lolly sticks (LS) to use as spacers; pastry brush; small paint brush; greaseproof paper; Ateco (or equivalent) icing nozzles 2 and 3; stiff card for template; 25mm (1in.) deep polystyrene foam and silver foil for lid support; 250mm (10in.) square silver cake board.

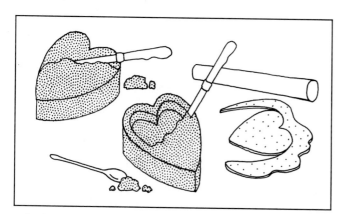

1. Cut the top of one cake flat, then turn over. Cut into top of other cake to a depth of about 25mm (1in.) and 15mm (½in.) in from the edge. Carefully scoop out the cake. Brush the inside with jam. Roll marzipan to 2 LS thick and cut the heart shape to fit. Apply.

2. Roll a strip of marzipan to 1 LS thick and apply, in two pieces, to inside sides.

Measure outside sides, from heart point to centre. Brush sides of both cakes with jam. Roll marzipan to 2 LS thick, cut to size, then apply (four pieces in all).

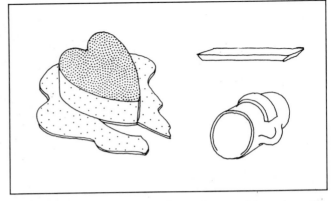

3. Brush top edge of hollowed cake with jam. Cut and apply two strips of marzipan to 1 LS thick.

Turn cake over on to dusted surface and brush with jam. Roll marzipan to 1 LS thick, lay cake on and cut round.

4. Roll marzipan to 2 LS thick. Brush top of flat cake with jam, lay it on marzipan and cut round.

Roll a piece of white fondant to 3 LS thick. Cut to 10mm ($\frac{3}{8}$in.) wide and 90mm ($3\frac{1}{2}$in.) long. Cut sloping ends as shown. Dust a straight-sided mug and carefully lay on the fondant. Leave to dry.

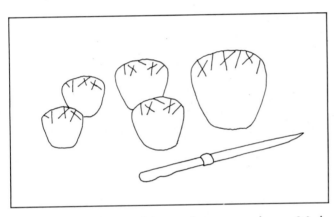

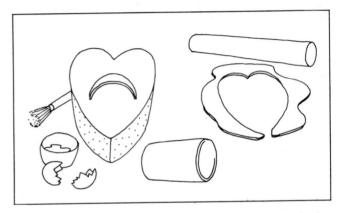

5. Model one white and four red stones, as shown. Mark criss-cross lines on surface with sharp knife.

Leave cakes, stones (on a dusted surface) and ring to dry for 48 hours.

6. Colour 220g (8oz) of fondant dark blue and the remainder pale blue. Roll dark blue to 2 LS thick and cover top of flat cake, using egg white to secure. Carefully position ring while fondant is still soft, press gently to indent, then remove and return to mug.

7. Using pale blue fondant cover sides of both cakes and back of lid, exactly as with marzipan, but using egg white instead of jam. Cover the top edge of the lid with two pieces at 1 LS thick.

8. Trace the medium-sized heart on page 106 on to stiff card then cut out the shape. To make gathered fabric inside lid, cut lengths of dark blue fondant 1 LS thick and 40mm (1½in.) deep. Gather on to the edge, brushed with egg white, and press on to base. Cut heart to 1 LS thick and position on base, covering edges of gathers.

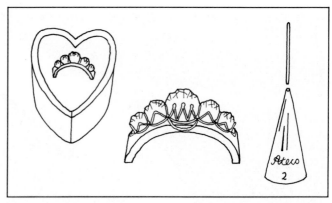

9. Roll remaining blue fondant to 2 LS thick. Cut two strips 10mm ($\frac{3}{8}$in.) wide and attach around top edge of flat cake. Cut two more 16mm ($\frac{5}{8}$in.) wide and attach to cover top edges of frill on lid.

10. Make the royal icing.

Paint the ring with gold. Dab a little silver and gold on the stones. Very carefully position ring, securing with dabs of icing. Position each stone with a dab of icing. With *No. 2 nozzle* pipe supports, as shown, around stones. When dry paint piping gold.

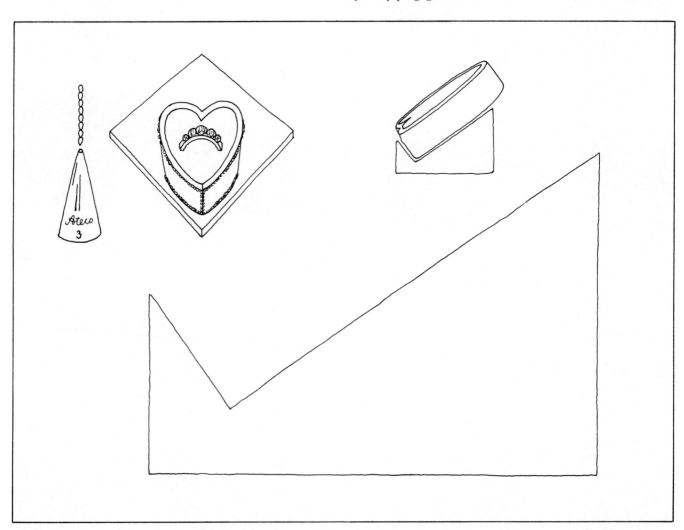

11. Position , with a blob of icing, the flat cake in corner of cake board. With pale blue icing and *No. 3 nozzle* pipe continuous dots along top edge, base and front seam of cake, then around top edge of lid. With dark blue icing pipe around heart inside the lid and around the inside edge of the flat cake.

12. Trace the support shape on to card, then use as a template. Cut two polystyrene supports. Cover neatly with silver foil, using glue or cellotape. Glue supports on to board, then position lid. Roll a little fondant to 1 LS thick. Cut hinges, attach then paint or pipe screw heads, as shown.

Wedding

Although this is not a traditional cake-decorating book I have departed only slightly from the conventionally designed wedding cake — the tiered effect seems appropriate; bride and groom are dressed in the customary attire and the overall hue is pale. As with the twenty-first birthday, it will probably be many decades before the 'white wedding' fades into the mists of time, if ever.

The steps are made from three square cakes: a 150mm (6in.), a 200mm (8in.) and a 250mm (10in.). Ingredients and quantities for these are given on page 127 and method for baking on page 6–7. Instructions for making royal icing, marzipan and fondant are on page 7. If you make your own fondant it will be easier to make the 2.250kg (5lb) in several batches, keeping each piece securely wrapped in cling film and in an air-tight container.

The cake will take a day to decorate, after the covering of marzipan and pieces of filigree have been left to dry for 48 hours. Piping the filigree fence is not difficult, but a little practice beforehand will give confidence if this kind of work is new to you. It is wise to make at least one more of each piece than is required.

Please read the General Notes on pages 6 to 9 before starting to decorate. Also read the step-by-step instructions and check the ingredient and equipment lists.

Ingredients for fondant and royal icing

2.250kg (5lb) icing sugar, plus 220g (8oz)
5 egg whites, plus 1
10 tblsp liquid glucose
flavouring (optional)
Also: 1.680kg (3¾lb) marzipan; warm sieved apricot jam; 50/50 mixture of cornflour and icing sugar in a dusting dredger; black, blue, flesh, red, lemon and gold food colouring.

Equipment

Mixing bowls; spoons; sieve; rolling pin; steel rule; sharp-pointed knife; lolly sticks (LS) as spacers; pastry brush; small paint brush; greaseproof paper; Ateco (or equivalent) icing nozzles 1, 2, 3, 4 and 13; tracing paper; stiff white card; waxed paper; cellotape; sharp-pointed scalpel; 330mm (13in.) square silver cake board.

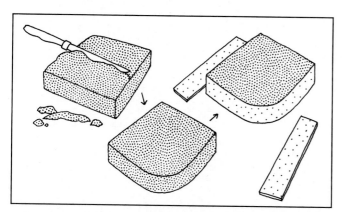

1. Slice the tops of the cakes flat, then turn over. Round off one corner of each. With marzipan at 2 LS thick, cover the cakes. Take the largest first, brush the sides with jam and apply marzipan — cover the two sides with the rounded corner in one piece.

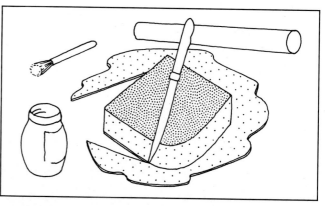

2. Brush the top with jam. Roll marzipan to 2 LS thick. Lay cake on top and carefully cut round. Repeat with medium and small cake. then leave all to dry for 48 hours. Meanwhile . . .

3. Make the royal icing. Trace the diagrams above on to pieces of tracing paper, then on to pieces of white card. Cellotape waxed paper over the drawings. Have ready three icing bags with *nozzles 1, 2* and *3* and white icing. Follow the directions and sequence given in the small diagrams. All the squiggly lines are piped with *No. 1*. The hearts and lines extending from them and the curved lines inside the small half circles and triangles are piped with *No. 2*. The outer lines and all straight lines are piped with *No. 3*. You will need one piece of **A**, one of **B**, two of **C** and four of **D**, but pipe one more of each in case of accidents. Leave all to dry for at least 24 hours.

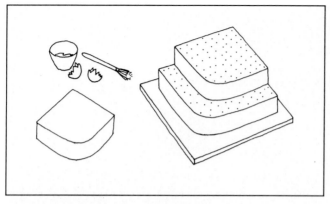

4. Roll white fondant to 2 LS thick. Cover all cake sides and top of the smallest cake exactly as for marzipan, but using egg white instead of jam. Position the largest cake on the board. Brush underneath middle cake with jam and position on top of large cake.

5. Brush underneath small cake and position on middle cake. Measure first and second steps. Cut pieces of fondant to fit, as shown. Trim corners when fondant has been applied.

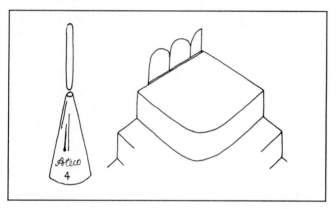

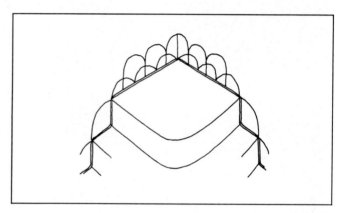

6. Carefully peel waxed paper from piped pieces. With *nozzle No. 4* pipe a line of icing along one straight edge of top cake. Gently press piece **A** on to the line. Hold or support the piece, back and front, until it feels secure. Repeat with other side.

7. Pipe a line in each corner and gently press **D**s in. Pipe a line down the back where **A** and **B** join in the corner. Pipe a line of continuous dots at base of **A** and **B**, then carefully press the two **C**s against the line. Hold for a little while.

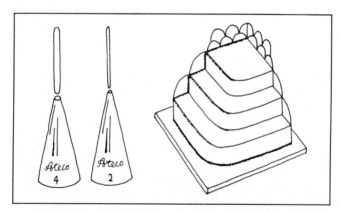

8. Pipe continuous dots along base of all pieces, then round base of cake. With *No. 2 nozzle* pipe lines of continuous dots on all fondant seams of cake.

9. Colour 170g (6oz) of fondant grey. Model the trousers and shoes, as shown, from 90g (3oz) of the grey. Position on the top step with egg white. Model white body from 60g (2oz) and position next to legs. Roll 90g (3oz) to 1 LS thick, cut a piece 200m x 120mm (8in. x 5in.). Gather, then attach to waist with egg white.

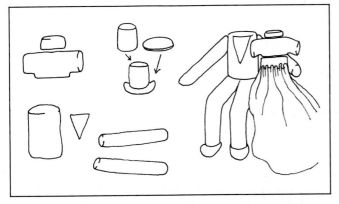

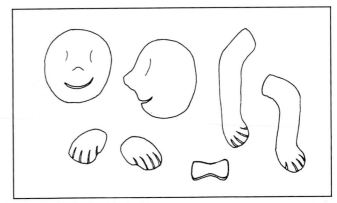

10. Attach 30g (1oz) to body for sleeves, as shown, and 15g (½oz) for neck. Model grey body from 45g (1½oz), then attach a small V-shaped white piece. Attach body to legs. Roll arms and attach one around bride. Use most of remaining grey to model hat, as shown, curling brim slightly at each side.

11. Model two heads, two arms and two hands from about 60g (2oz) of flesh coloured fondant. Mark smiling mouths and fingers with knife, then position all pieces. Model a little bow-tie with remaining grey fondant, then attach.

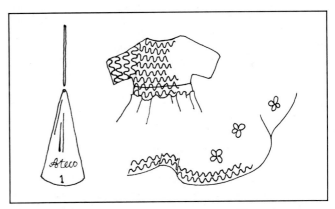

12. Roll about 60g (2oz) of white fondant to 1 LS thick and cut to shape shown. Brush egg white on bride's head, then carefully attach veil. Paint eyes on both faces; rosy cheeks and lips on bride.

(When piping the figures, take care not to knock the filigree fencing.)

13.. With *No. 1 nozzle* and white icing, pipe wavy lines over dress bodice, three rows on dress hem and two rows on veil hem. Pipe little four-petalled flowers on dress and veil, then wavy lines around head. With the same nozzle and pale blue icing, pipe two more wavy lines around dress and veil hems, and on bodice.

14. Pipe blue dots in centre of flowers and dots in white lines of hems, as shown.

Pipe (with same nozzle) a ring on bride's and groom's finger.

Using appropriate coloured icing, pipe hair on both heads, then position hat on groom.

15. With lemon icing and *No. 13 nozzle* pipe little flowers on bride's head-dress and on groom's lapel.

Paint the rings and lines on fondant seams with gold.

First wedding anniversary

On seeing this chunk of wood with initials romantically carved, and knowing it was to celebrate a first wedding anniversary, my husband jokingly remarked, "Ah, the rot hasn't set in yet!"

The log is made from a 200mm (8in.) square cake. The ingredients and quantities for this are given on page 127 and the method for baking is on page 6–7. Instructions for making royal icing, marzipan and fondant are on page 7. If you are making your own fondant the amount required, 560g (1¼lb), is not large and so can be made in one go, but remember to keep it securely wrapped in cling film until required.

The cake is very easy to decorate and, after allowing the marzipan to dry for 48 hours, can be completed in a day. This was my first attempt at piping 'real' flowers. It proved much easier than I thought, so other novices will not find it at all difficult. Just a little practice is necessary beforehand.

Please read the General Notes on pages 6 to 9 before starting to decorate. Also read through the step-by-step instructions and check the ingredient and equipment lists.

Ingredients for fondant and royal icing

560g (1¼lb) icing sugar, plus 170g (6oz)
1¼ egg whites, plus ¾
2½ tblsp liquid glucose
flavouring (optional)
Also: 560g (1¼lb) marzipan; warm sieved apricot jam; 50/50 mixture of cornflour and icing sugar in a dusting dredger; brown, red, yellow and black food colouring.

Equipment

Mixing bowls; spoons; sieve; rolling pin; steel rule; sharp-pointed knife; lolly sticks (LS) as spacers; pastry brush; small paint brush; greaseproof paper; Ateco (or equivalent) icing nozzles 2 and 60; 250mm (10in.) round silver cake board; waxed paper; flat flower nail; 1 birthday cake candle.

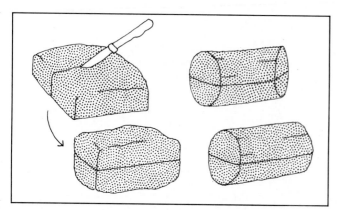

1. Cut the cake in half, and join the two flat sides together with jam and a slice of marzipan. Round the cake off, keeping a flat base, and cut one of the ends to slope inwards.

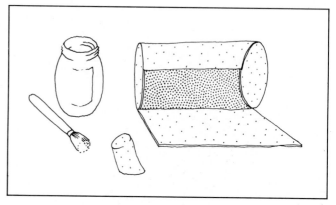

2. Brush the cake with jam. Roll the marzipan to 2 LS thick. Cover the ends first, then the top and sides in one piece, as shown. Model a branch and leave both to dry for 48 hours.

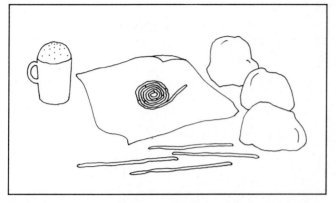

3. Position the log on the cake board. Divide the fondant into three and colour medium brown, yellowy brown and reddy brown. Dust a piece of waxed paper. Start with a small blob of fondant in the centre. Roll thin uneven strips of colour and press round to form a circle.

4. Continue until the circle is roughly the size of log side, then roll to 2 LS thick. Brush the marzipan with egg white, apply the circle of fondant and trim the edges. Repeat other side. Make small circle, with thinner strips, for the branch.

5. Knead remaining fondant with trimmings. Add more brown colouring and roll to 2 LS thick. Brush marzipan with egg white. With help of rolling pin, apply the fondant to the log. Trim edges. Cover the branch and attach to log with icing. Attach circle and trim. Brush streaks of brown colour across the bark.

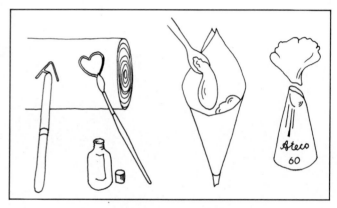

6. Mark initials and hearts with round bladed knife. Paint inside the marks with black.

Make the 170g (6oz) of royal icing. Colour half pale yellow. Put one teaspoon each of white and yellow icing in an icing bag with *nozzle No. 60.*

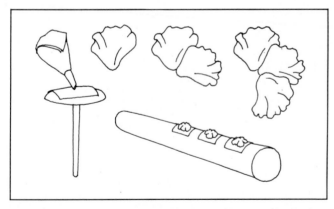

7. Attach a 25mm (1in.) square of waxed paper to the flower nail with a dab of icing. Rest the thick end of the nozzle in the centre and pipe a petal. Continue twisting the nail round and piping petals, five or six. Remove paper with flower and leave to dry on the rolling pin.

8. Pipe 22 flowers for the rolling pin. Leave 8 more to dry on a flat surface. Leave all to dry for 3 hours. Attach flowers with a dab of icing, curved ones on log. With *No. 2 nozzle* pipe yellow dots in each flower centre. Stick candle in, as shown, and pipe several dots round base.

Christening

This cake was originally made to commemorate the birth of Prince Harry. I have not included the Union Jack back-drop in the instructions, so your cot will simply stand in the centre of the base cake. You can replace the crown on the cushion with a gold or silver rattle. The crown on the side of the cot can be replaced by a small plaque with the child's name. If the child is a girl, pink colouring can be used instead of blue. Do make sure that the gold or silver is the edible type of food colouring, unless you wish to keep the rattle, cushion and plaque as mementos.

The cot is made from a 200mm (8in.) square cake and the base from a 250mm (10in.) square. Ingredients and quantities for these are given on page 127 and the method for baking on page 6–7. Instructions for making royal icing, marzipan and fondant are given on page 7. If you are making your own fondant (list of ingredients given on this page), it will be easier to make the 1.570kg (3½lb) in two or three batches, keeping it securely wrapped in cling film and in an airtight container.

The cake will take two or three days to decorate, after the covering of marzipan has been left to dry for 48 hours.

Please read the General Notes on pages 6 to 9 before starting to decorate. Read also the step-by-step instructions and check the ingredient and equipment lists.

Ingredients for fondant and royal icing

1.570kg (3½lb) icing sugar, plus 220g (8oz)
3½ egg whites, plus 1
7 tblsp liquid glucose
flavouring (optional)
Also: 1.120kg (2½lb) marzipan; warm sieved apricot jam; 50/50 mixture of cornflour and icing sugar in a dusting dredger; food colouring – royal and turquoise blues or rose and salmon pinks, flesh, brown and gold or silver; edible silver balls.

Equipment

Mixing bowls; spoons; sieve; rolling pin; steel rule; sharp-pointed knife; lolly sticks (LS) to use as spacers; pastry brush; small paint brush; 'spade' cocktail cutter; greaseproof paper; Ateco (or equivalent) icing nozzles 1, 2, 3 and 13; 360mm (14in.) square silver cake board.

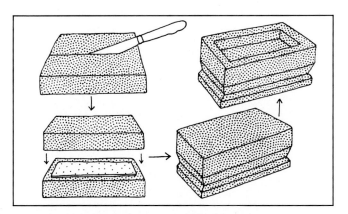

1. Cut the smaller cake in half, then sandwich together with jam and marzipan. Shape the bottom half as shown, cutting a slope in about 10mm (½in.), then out again. Measure 10mm (½in.) in from each edge on the top and scoop out a rectangle about 20mm (¾in.) deep.

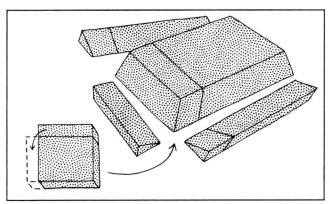

2. Cut a 50mm (2in.) strip from the larger cake. Attach the strip, using jam and marzipan, to one of the short sides and trim to make a rectangle 200mm x 300mm (8in. x 12in.). Measure 10mm (½in.) in from each of the four top edges and cut slopes, as shown.

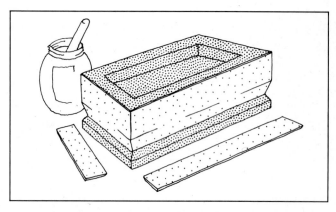

3. Measure the cot sides, then brush with the warm sieved jam. Roll marzipan to 2 LS thick and cut to fit, each side in two pieces, as shown.

Line the inside and top with marzipan 1 LS thick.

4. Brush the sides of the base cake with jam. Roll the marzipan to 2 LS thick, cut to fit, then apply. Repeat for top of cake.

Leave base and top to dry for 48 hours.

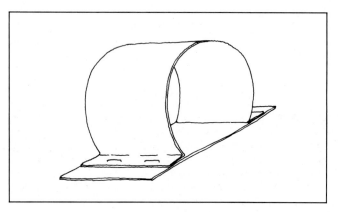

5. Meanwhile, make a support for the cot hood – cut a strip of card 140mm (5½in.) long. Cut another one 75mm (3in.) wide and 240mm (9in.) long. Bend the longest card so that it fits over across the cot, then staple or cellotape the bent card to the straight piece, as shown.

6. Take 670g (1½lb) of fondant and colour pale turquoise/rose pink. Roll a piece for the cot hood to 2 LS thick. (Wrap the remainder in cling film and place in an airtight container.)

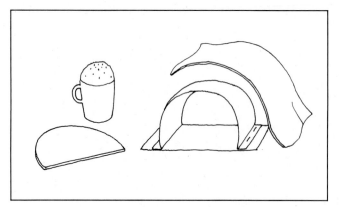

7. Lay the card hood on its back, on the fondant, and cut round – this will be the hood back. Leave to dry on a dusted surface. Cut fondant to fit over the card, dust card liberally, then carefully lay fondant on top.

Leave the hood to dry with the marzipanned cakes.

8. Cover the cot with the turquoise/rose fondant, as with marzipan (caption 4), but using egg white to secure instead of jam. Do not cover flat bottom of inside cot.

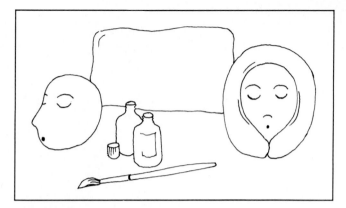

9. Add a drop of flesh to a little white fondant and model baby's head, as shown. Paint eyes and lips. Use watered pink for rosy cheeks. Make a little white shawl, as shown, and position around head. Model the pale royal blue/salmon pillow and position in the cot. Place baby's head on pillow, securing with egg white.

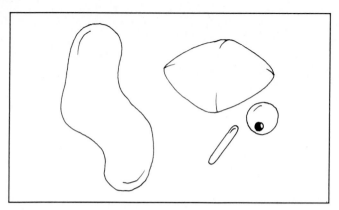

10. Model body shape, as shown, then position in cot. Model royal blue/deep rose cushion and white rattle, as shown. Pierce a hole in rattle ball with paint brush handle, push rattle handle in, with a dab of egg white, when dry.

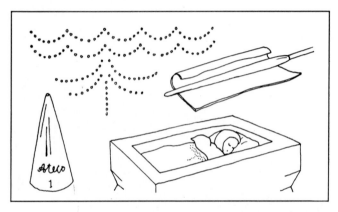

11. Roll some pale royal blue/salmon fondant to 1 LS thick and cut a blanket. Using point of *No. 1 nozzle*, make the pattern, as shown, then lay blanket over baby. Roll a piece of white fondant to 1 LS thick, curl one edge over paint brush handle, then position as shown.

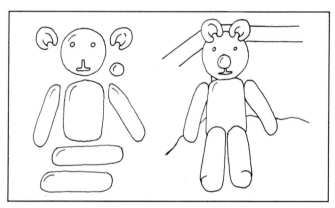

12. Colour some fondant brown and model little teddy bear, in pieces, as shown. Mark mouth with blunt edge of knife, and the eyes with paint brush handle. Stick head to body with egg white, then position in corner of cot. Position legs and arms, securing with egg white.

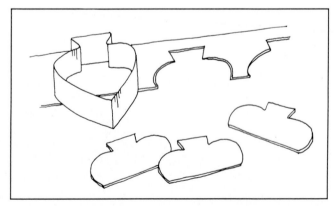

13. Using blue/pink fondant trimmings, roll to 1 LS thick and cut into strips. Cut out shapes, as shown, with 'spade' cocktail cutter. Attach to bottom edge of cot with egg white. Using same fondant 1 LS thick, cut plaque for baby's name.

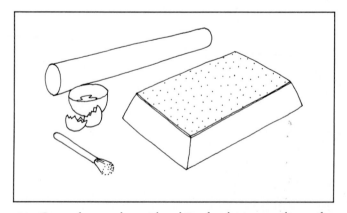

14. Cover base cake with white fondant, exactly as for marzipan (caption 5) but using a thin film of egg white to secure side pieces, instead of jam. Position on silver board.

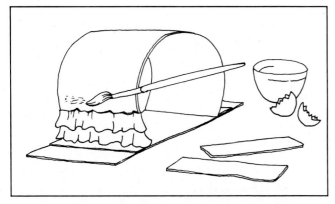

15. While hood is still on card support, attach frills. Roll white fondant to 1 LS thick. Cut into strips 20mm (¾in.) wide and roughly same length as hood. Nip along each strip with thumb and forefinger to make fondant thinner. Paint a line of egg white along hood, as shown. Make gathers while attaching strip.

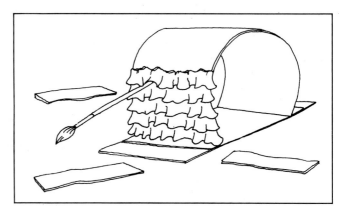

16. Pull gathers out with paint brush handle, as shown. Work up to hood top, then repeat with other side and back. Stick narrow strips of soft fondant on to cot edge, then very carefully position hood. Make frill to go round cot (in pieces). Attach as before, trimming away excess fondant at top edge.

17. With *No. 13 nozzle* and blue/pink icing pipe around edge and inside of hood, continue around top of cot frill. Pipe three lines on top of hood, dropping silver balls on to middle line while icing is still wet. Pipe down corner seams of cot.

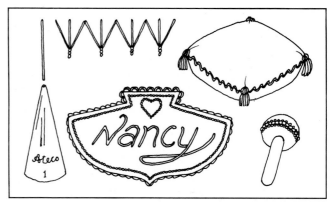

18. With *No. 1 nozzle* and white icing, pipe braid and tassels on cushion, tassels over cot frill, name of child on plaque, and decoration, as shown, on plaque and rattle. When the icing has dried, paint with gold or silver. Also paint rattle handle.

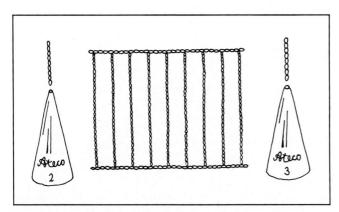

19. With *No. 2 nozzle* and alternate pale and dark blue/pink icing, pipe lines of continuous dots and down sides of base cake, at 10mm (½in.) intervals. With *No. 3 nozzle* pipe dark blue/pink around bottom, and white around top edge.

20. Position cot, at an angle, on the base cake and cushion with rattle at the side. Attach plaque to the side of the cot with a dab of icing.

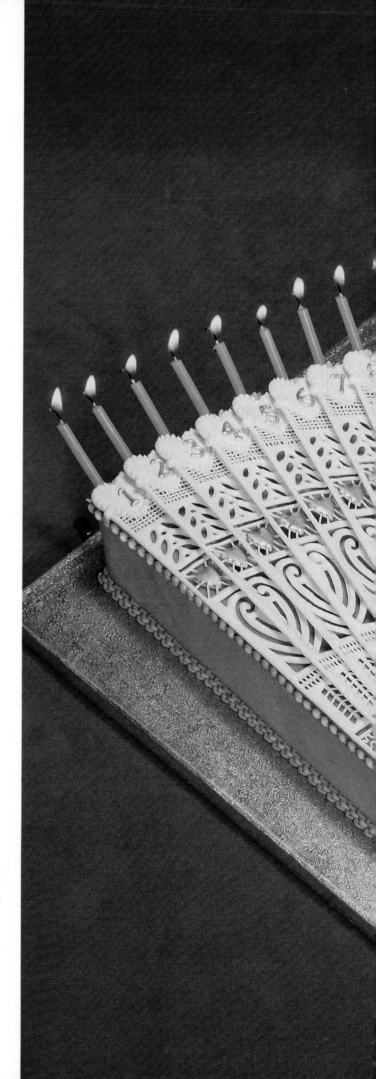

The basic shape of this silver (25th) wedding anniversary cake can be used for other anniversaries. The filigree fan piece will have to be redrawn, making it slightly narrower for more years and wider for fewer years.

Here is a list of traditional anniversary names: ten — tin; eleven — steel; twelve — silk; thirteen — lace; fourteen — ivory; fifteen — crystal; twenty — china; twenty-five — silver; thirty — pearl; thirty-five — coral; forty — ruby; forty-five — sapphire; fifty — golden; sixty — diamond.

36

Wedding anniversaries

This ornate fan spanning twenty-five years is in the traditional mode. The idea can be used for any anniversary, after the tenth, by altering the colour scheme and the width and number of fan pieces. It would probably be too difficult to fit any more than fifty pieces on the cake. I have drawn up a list of traditional anniversaries which is given on page 36.

Making the fan pieces is not difficult, but time and patience are needed. Once set, however, the pieces are extremely fragile. It is best to slide them gently from one surface to another where possible; or very carefully pick up in the middle with thumb and forefinger. If they do break, and unless they are completely shattered, a little blob of runny icing on the break will be enough to secure. In the instructions I have suggested making more than the required number, just in case.

The base is made from a 300 (12in.) and 130mm (5in.) square cake. Ingredients for these are given on page 127 and the method of baking, along with instructions for royal icing, marzipan and fondant, are given on page 6–7. If you make your own fondant, it will be easier to make the 1.340kg (3lb) in three batches, keeping each piece securely wrapped in cling film and in an airtight container until required.

Please read the General Notes on pages 6 to 9 before starting to decorate the cake. Also read through the step-by-step instructions and check the ingredient and equiment lists.

Ingredients for fondant and royal icing

1.340kg (3lb) icing sugar, plus 450g (1lb)
3 egg whites, plus 2
6 tblsp liquid glucose
flavouring (optional)
Also: 1.120kg (2½lb) marzipan; warm sieved apricot jam; 50/50 mixture of icing sugar and cornflour in a dusting dredger; blue, black, flesh and silver food colour; silver balls.

Equipment

Mixing bowls; spoons; sieve; rolling pin; steel rule; sharp-pointed knife; lolly sticks (LS) as spacers; pastry brush; small paint brush; greaseproof paper; Ateco (or equivalent) 1, 2, 3 and 4; stiff white card; adhesive tape; tracing paper; HB graphite pencil; skewer; waxed paper; coloured-headed sewing pins; 25 candles and holders; oil-based silver paint; 400mm (16in.) square silver cake board.

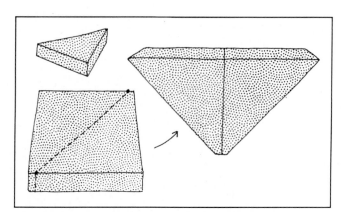

1. Slice the tops of the cakes flat. Cut the small cake across diagonally (only one half is used). Cut the large cake diagonally, as shown, 12mm (½in.) from the two opposite corners. Stick the two pieces together with jam and a strip of marzipan.

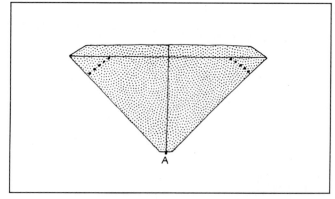

2. From the centre bottom, **A**, measure a 330mm (13in.) curve coming in from the edges. Mark the curve with the sewing pins, then carefully cut the curves off.

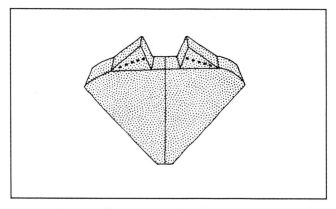

3. Trim the cut-off corners so they fit at the top of the fan, then stick them with jam and marzipan. Continue to measure, mark and trim the 330mm (13in.) curve. Fill the top gap with pieces from the last trim.

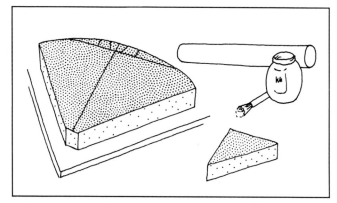

4. Carefully position the cake on the board. Measure the cake sides, then brush with jam. Roll marzipan to 2 LS thick, cut to fit, then apply. Brush cake top. Apply marzipan (2 LS thick) with help of a rolling pin. Neatly trim edges. Cover small cake. Leave both to dry for 48 hours. Meanwhile, follow caption 5 on page 40.

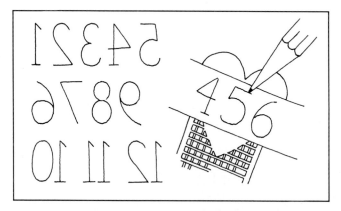

6. Using the HB graphite (not lead) pencil, trace the above numbers on to a strip of tracing paper. Carefully arrange the 25 fan pieces in pairs on the table. Turn the paper over and very carefully trace each number on to a heart. (You may be able to draw the numbers freehand, instead of tracing.)

7. With *No. 2 nozzle* pipe the numbers. Pipe dots around each heart. Then leave to dry.

Trace **Congratulations** on to one of the solid fan pieces. With *No. 2*, pipe over the pencilled letters.

When dry, carefully paint numbers, little hearts and lettering silver. Leave to dry.

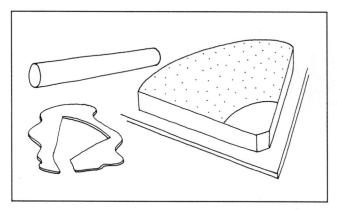

8. Take 1.120kg (2½lb) of fondant. Cover the large cake sides with white fondant at 2 LS thick, exactly as for marzipan, but using egg white instead of jam. Roll a piece of fondant to 2 LS thick and cut a 100mm (4in.) arc to fit base of fan, as shown.

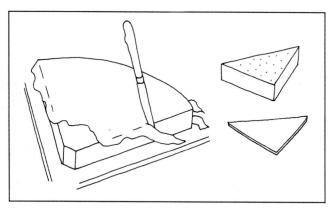

9. Colour remaining fondant blue. Roll to 2 LS thick and to roughly the shape of the fan. Brush a thin film of egg white on marzipan and apply fondant with the help of rolling pin. Trim edges. Add 90g (3oz) of white fondant to blue trimmings and cover the small cake.

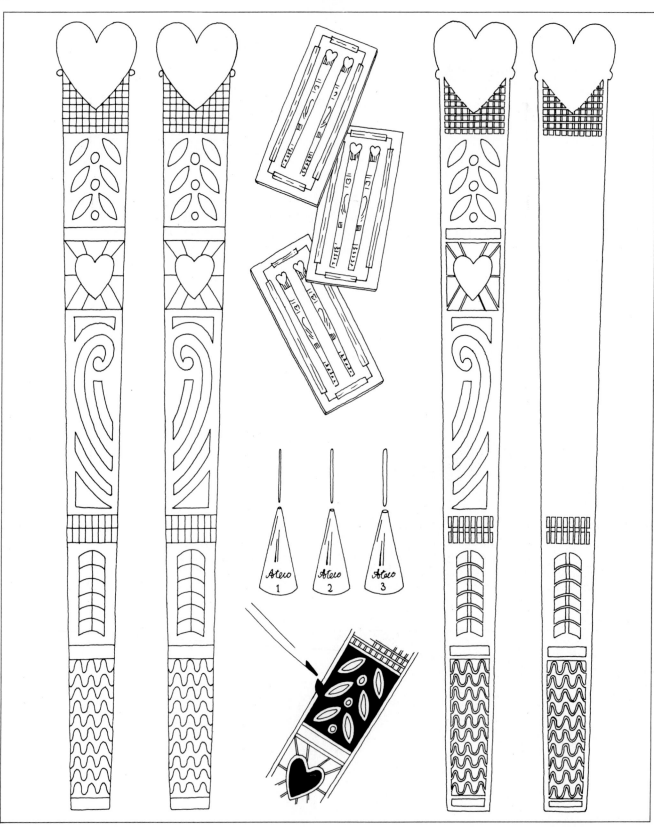

5. Trace the above two fan pieces on to three pieces of stiff white card, and then tape waxed paper over the drawings. Pipe the outer line and large heart with *No. 3 nozzle*; the ten horizontal and one vertical lines with *No. 2 nozzle* and the remainder with *No. 1*. Using a skewer, fill in the areas shown with watered icing. Leave the six pieces to dry for about three hours, then carefully remove the tape and leave them on a flat surface (still on the waxed paper) to dry overnight. Repeat until 28 pieces have been piped. Pipe two more pieces, filling in the areas shown. When the first pieces are dry, peel off the waxed paper. Leave underside to dry.

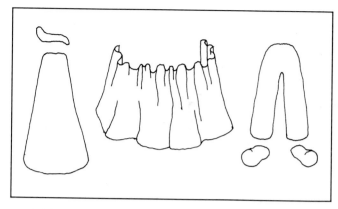

10. Make a cone, as shown, about 70mm (2¾in.) high, with remaining blue trimmings. Attach to little cake with egg white. Colour 45g (1½oz) pale blue (keep some for arms), attach little collar, then roll to 1 LS thick, gather and attach skirt. Colour 30g (1oz) grey, model and attach shoes, and trousers.

11. Model the body and attach shirt front and collar, as shown. Attach body to legs. Colour a little fondant flesh, model the heads, paint eyes, then attach. Model and attach arms and hands. Support joined hands until position is secure. With *No. 1* and white icing, pipe hair and decorations on dress.

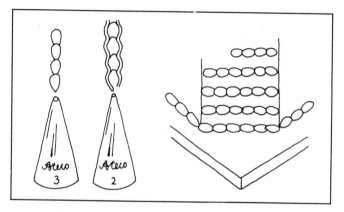

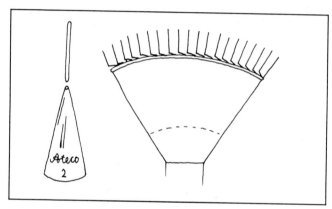

12. With *No. 3* and blue icing, pipe continuous dots around top of little cake. With white and *No. 2* follow top and bottom of blue line. Paint part of dress decorations and hair silver. With *No. 3* and white icing, pipe continuous dots around base of fan, around fondant seam at the top, and eight lines at point of fan, as shown.

13. Very carefully arrange fan pieces on cake. With white icing and *No. 2 nozzle* secure the pieces at the bottom with neat lines and, at the top, gently push the nozzle underneath each heart and pipe as large a blob as possible.
 Mark a circle 40mm (1½in.) from both sides.

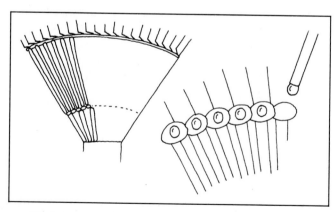

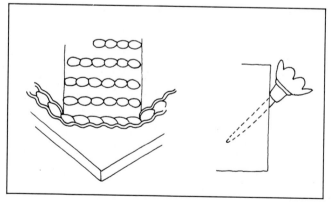

14. With *No. 3* and blue icing, pipe lines to the circle, then pipe the circle with a line of continuous dots. With *No. 4* pipe large dots to cover the lines, securing the fan pieces – place a silver ball on each dot (use a straw to suck the ball, then release as it touches icing). Pipe nine lines to the fan point.

15. With *No. 2* and blue icing, follow top and bottom of continuous dots around base of cake. Position small cake and, with *No. 3*, pipe continuous dots around base. Paint four candle holders silver, then push into cake. Secure all candles in holders then push into fan, at an angle, as shown.

Reconciliation

Second and even third marriages to the same partner occasionally hit the headlines; but breakdown and reconciliation within a marriage are probably much more frequent. This cake can be made for such an occasion. The wall symbolises the barrier which has built up between the couple – they are now in the process of taking it down.

The wall and base are made from one 180mm (7in.) square cake and one 200mm (8in.) round cake. Ingredients and quantities for these are given on page 127 method for baking on page 6–7. Instructions for making royal icing, marzipan and fondant are on page 7. If you make your own fondant, you may find it easier to make the 1.450kg (3¼lb) in three of four batches, keeping the pieces securely wrapped in cling film and in an airtight container until required.

The cake can be decorated in one to two days, after the covering of marzipan has been left to dry for 48 hours. The wall is made by cutting two pieces from the square cake. Cutting without crumbling can be tricky, so it helps to have a very sharp knife. If bits of cake do fall out they can be pressed back in, so long as the cake is very moist, or encouraged to stick with a smear of jam.

Please read the General Notes on page 6 to 9 before starting to decorate. Also read through the step-by-step instructions and check the ingredient and equipment lists.

Ingredients for fondant and royal icing

1.450kg (3¼lb) icing sugar, plus 60g (2oz)
3¼ egg whites, plus ¼
6½ tblsp liquid glucose
flavouring (optional)
Also: 1.120kg (2½lb) marzipan; warm sieved apricot jam; 50/50 mixture of cornflour and icing sugar in a dusting dredger; green, red, orange, yellow, flesh, blue and brown food colouring.

Equipment

Mixing bowls; spoons; sieve; rolling pin; steel rule; sharp-pointed knife; lolly sticks (LS) as spacers; pastry brush; greaseproof paper; Ateco (or equivalent) icing nozzles 1, 2 and 101; 250mm (10in.) round silver cake board.

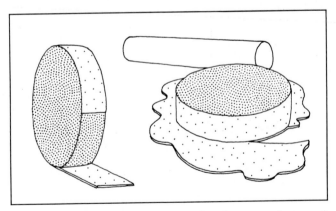

1. Slice the tops of the two cakes flat, then turn the round one over. Measure depth and circumference of round cake, brush sides with jam then roll marzipan to 2 LS thick. Cut to fit, and roll the cake along, as shown. Brush top of cake with jam, roll marzipan to 2 LS thick, position cake and cut round.

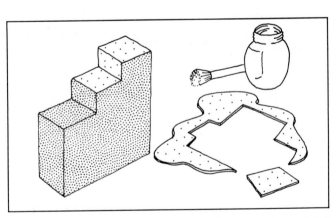

2. Cut steps from the square cake – first cut, 50mm (2in.) from edge, 300mm (1¼in.) down; then 50mm (2in.) across, 25mm (1in.) down; then 80mm (3in.) across.

Measure each step and the sides of the cake. Cover with marzipan as described for round cake, then cover top. Leave both cakes to dry for 48 hours.

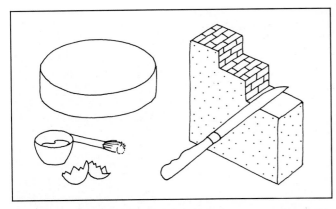

3. Colour 670g (1½lb) of fondant green. Cover round cake exactly as for marzipan, but, using egg white instead of jam. Add 450g (1lb) of fondant to trimmings and mix in red colour. Cover wall exactly as for marzipan, marking bricks with blunt edge of knife after application of each piece.

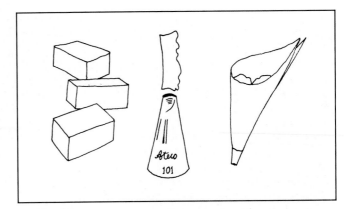

4. Cut nine bricks, 5 LS thick, from trimmings. Make the royal icing. Using *nozzle No 101* put a teaspoon of orange and one of white in the icing bag – place the orange towards the narrow end of the nozzle. Pipe flowers around edge of green cake, one a little higher, then lower, than the previous one . . .

5. . . . With wide end of nozzle against the cake, move top of nozzle round slightly for first petal, then move nozzle from one side of petal to the other three times, like wavy folds. When ending in centre, push the nozzle in slightly, then pull away to break icing.

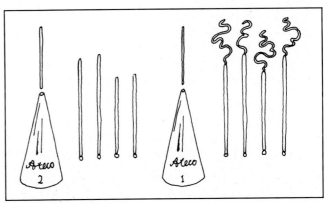

6. Refill an icing bag with same colour, this time placing white at narrow end of nozzle. Pipe flowers on wall. With green icing and *nozzle No 2* pipe flower stems, as shown, then continue stems with *No 1*.

Colour 110g (4oz) of fondant yellow and 110g (4oz) flesh.

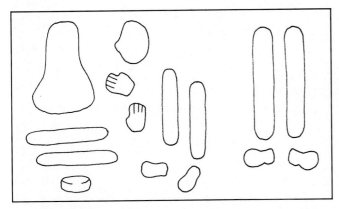

7. Model lady's body, as shown. Attach to wall with icing and support until secure. Attach collar and arms with egg white. Model hands and head. Attach as shown, one hand on a brick. Model and attach shoes and legs.

Model man's yellow shoes, then position. Add brown to brick trimmings, model trousers and attach to wall.

8. Colour 90g (3oz) of fondant blue. Model and attach body, collar and arms – one arm over a brick, as shown. Model and attach head and hands. Secure loose bricks to cake with icing. Paint eyes as shown. With *No 1 nozzle* and appropriate coloured icing, pipe hair.

44

Retirement

Retirement used to be synonymous with quiet contentment: slippers, feet up, pottering in the garden, knitting by the fire, reading and other gentle pursuits. Now, health (and funds) permitting, it usually denotes the onset of a life full of activity and new challenges. As water sports have become so popular I have used this theme to suggest freedom and adventure.

The sea is made from a 200mm (8in.) round cake. The ingredients and quantities for this are given on page 127 and the method for baking on page 6–7. Instructions for making royal icing, marzipan and fondant are given on page 7. If you make your own fondant, you may find it easier to make the 670g (1½lb) in two batches, keeping each securely wrapped in cling film and in an airtight box until required.

The cake design is simple. It can be decorated in a day, after the covering of marzipan and the sail have been left to dry for 48 hours. The wave effect around the cake is made by laying three colours, blue, white and mauve, together and pushing one colour into the other at intervals with the fingers. The fondant is then rolled out flat.

Please read the General Notes on pages 6 to 9 before starting to decorate. Also read through the step-by-step instructions and check the ingredients and equipment lists.

Ingredients for fondant and royal icing

670g (1½lb) icing sugar, plus 60g (2oz)
1½ eggs, plus ¼
3 tblsp liquid glucose
flavouring (optional)
Also: 450g (1lb) marzipan; warm sieved apricot jam; 50/50 mixture of cornflour and icing sugar in a dusting dredger; blue, mauve, flesh and gold food colouring.

Equipment

Mixing bowls; spoons; sieve; rolling pin; steel rule; sharp-pointed knife; lolly sticks (LS) as spacers; pastry brush; small paint brush; greaseproof paper; Ateco (or equivalent) icing nozzles 1, 2 and 4; waxed paper; 250mm (10in.) round silver cake board.

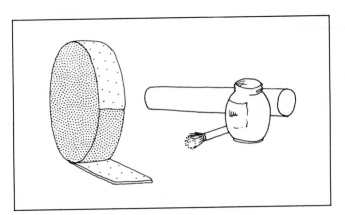

1. Slice the top of the cake flat and turn over. Measure depth and circumference. Roll marzipan to 2 LS thick, then cut a piece to fit round the sides. Brush sides with jam and roll the cake along, as shown.

2. Brush the cake top with jam. Roll marzipan to 2 LS thick, lay the cake on then cut round, as shown. Leave to dry for 48 hours.

Meanwhile mix the royal icing and make the sail.

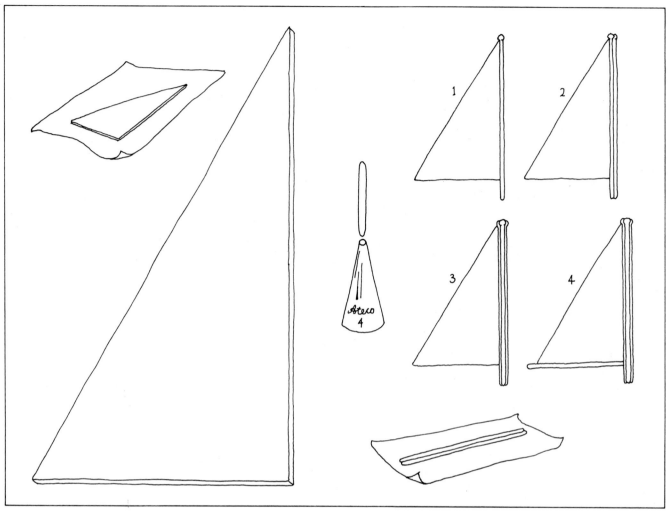

3. Take 60g (2oz) of fondant and roll to 1 LS thick. Cut the sail, horizontal side 75mm (3in.) and vertical side 125mm (5in.) Lay it carefully on a piece of waxed paper.

4. With *nozzle No 4* pipe lines as shown in the diagram — three lines on vertical side, ending in three blobs at the top and one line along the base. On another piece of waxed paper pipe a double line 135mm (5¼in.) long. Leave sail, and support to dry on a flat surface.

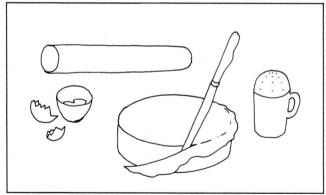

5. Take 450g (1lb) of fondant. Colour 170g (6oz) blue, 170g (6oz) mauve and leave the remainder white. Take just over half of each piece, roll lightly together as described on previous page, then roll to 2 LS thick and cut a piece to fit around cake. Secure with a thin film of egg white.

6. Lightly mix trimmings with remaining colours. Roll to 2 LS thick. Brush a thin film of egg white on cake top, lay fondant on, and neatly trim the edges. Secure cake to silver board with a smear of icing.

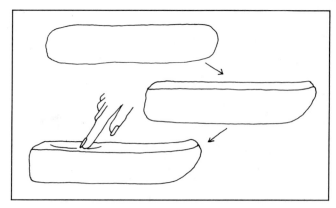

7. Add 90g (3oz) of fondant to trimmings from sail. Make a roll roughly 150mm (6in.) long, then form it into a boat shape, as shown. Push finger into end to make a hollow about 50mm (2in.) long. Position boat on cake, securing with egg white.

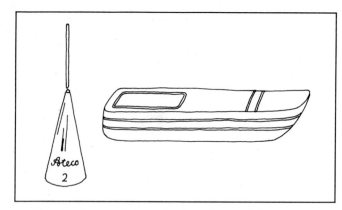

8. Tip the front of the cake board up, slide a tin or jar underneath. With No 2 nozzle and white icing pipe two parallel lines along side of boat. Repeat with other side and back. Pipe two lines across front of boat, and a line round indented area.

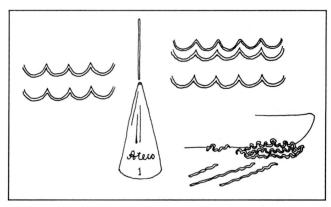

9. With the same nozzle, pipe two wavy lines around top of cake. With nozzle No 1 follow the top wavy line. Pipe squiggles, as shown on the photograph, along sides of the boat to suggest foam.

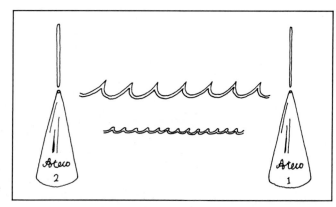

10. Roll some blue trimmings to 1 LS thick. Cut a strip, slightly curved, 20mm (¾in.) deep and 150mm (6in.) long. With nozzle No 2 pipe **HAPPY RETIREMENT** or an appropriate message. Pipe little waves above the lettering. With No 1 nozzle pipe a chain round the edge of the fondant. Paint the sail supports gold.

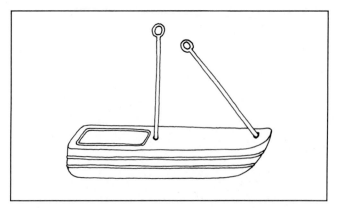

11. Using a skewer or knitting needle, carefully make a slanting hole at the front of the boat, then one in the centre 75mm (3in.) from the front. Carefully push sail in centre hole, allowing it to rest on boat side. Push double line in to rest on sail. With No 2 pipe two circles around base of poles.

12. Pipe three blobs at top of double line. Pipe three lines at both sides of centre circles and two lines from end of the sail to back of boat. When dry paint all lines gold. Model the figure pieces as shown, then assemble in boat with egg white. Paint eyes. Pipe neck tie with No 2.

Fun Events

Teenage party

This cake is for those parents who are brave enough to arrange a teenage party and extend a warm welcome to the friends of their teenage offspring.

The house is made from three 150mm (6in.) square cakes. Ingredients are given on page 127 and the method for baking on page 6–7. Instructions for making royal icing, marzipan and fondant are on page 7. If you make your own fondant, it will be easier to make the 1.120kg (2½lb) in two lots.

The cake will take one to two days to decorate, after the marzipan has been left to dry for 48 hours.

Please read the General Notes on pages 6 to 9 before starting to decorate. Also read through the step-by-step instructions and check the ingredient and equipment lists.

Ingredients for fondant and royal icing

1.120kg (2½lb) icing sugar, plus 110g (4oz)
2½ egg whites, plus ½
5 tblsp liquid glucose
flavouring (optional)
Also: 1.120kg (2½lb) marzipan; warm sieved apricot jam; 50/50 mixture of cornflour and icing sugar in a dusting dredger; bright red, brown, yellow, blue and flesh colouring.

Equipment

Mixing bowls; spoons; sieve; rolling pin; steel rule; sharp-pointed knife; lolly sticks (LS) to use as spacers; pastry brush; small paint brush; greaseproof paper; Ateco (or equivalent) icing nozzles 1, 2, 13 and 65; 200mm (10in.) square silver cake board.

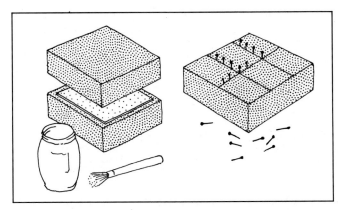

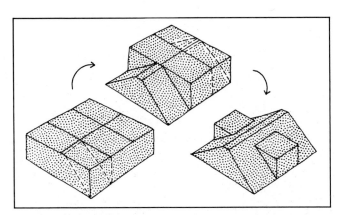

1. Slice the tops of the cakes flat. Brush the top of one and the underside of another with jam, then sandwich together with a piece of marzipan 1 LS thick. Divide the roof (third cake) into six sections, marking with coloured headed pins, as shown.

2. Leaving a narrow ridge on top of the roof, cut the four sloping sides, as shown. Continue the slope down a little way on the two centre pieces, then slice flat for the top of the dorma windows, as shown. (If bits of the cake have broken off, try to stick them back or fill the holes with marzipan.)

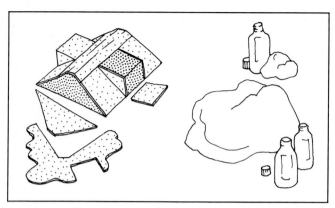

3. Keep one of the cut-away slopes and cut into a wedge – this will help to support the roof. Roll the marzipan to 2 LS thick, brush sides of house with jam, lay it on the marzipan, then cut to fit. Continue until all sides and top are covered.

4. Apply marzipan to all roof surfaces, including under-side. Cover the wedge with marzipan 1 LS thick. Leave everything to dry for 48 hours.

Take 900g (2lb) of fondant, break off about 75g (2½oz), colour yellow, then cover and put to one side. Colour remaining fondant brick (bright red and brown).

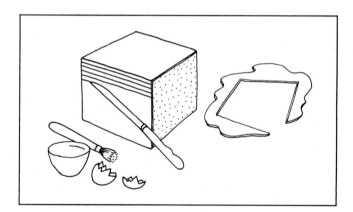

5. Cover the house, as with marzipan, caption 3, but using egg white instead of jam. Mark each wall with bricks directly after application – I used a long sharp knife for the horizontal lines and an artist's palette knife for the vertical lines. Position the house on the silver board.

6. Cover the under-side of the roof, then gable ends, then the dorma cheeks, marking bricks as before. Cover wedge with fondant 1 LS thick. Roll the yellow fondant to 1 LS thick, cut windows of varying sizes, and a door shape. Attach with egg white.

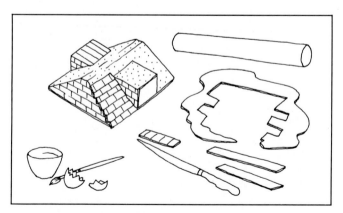

7. Add brown to remaining yellow fondant, roll to 2 LS thick and cut a door. Leave to dry on a dusted surface. Model a chimney with remaining brick fondant. Mark bricks and paint brown circle on top. Leave to dry. Take about 110g (4oz) of fondant and colour blue.

8. Roll to 1 LS thick and cut two pieces to fit dorma roofs. Indent lines with blunt edge of knife, then attach with egg white. Cut strips 20mm (¾in.) wide, mark lines and, starting from bottom, attach to roof, each strip overlapping half of the previous one. Complete both sides of roof stopping at top ridge.

IF YOU MUST RAISE THE ROOF
———— DO IT QUIETLY !!!

9. Attach chimney with egg white. Roll a piece of blue fondant for roof ridge and attach. Make the 110g (4oz) of royal icing. Roll some blue fondant to 1 LS thick, cut to fit two sides of the silver board. With *No. 1 nozzle* and yellow icing, pipe **IF YOU MUST RAISE THE ROOF   DO IT QUIETLY!!!**

10. With *No. 2 nozzle* and brown icing, pipe windows, door and two lines on fondant seam round top of house. Pipe two climbers up the walls. Position door with a line of icing. With *No. 65* and green icing, pipe small leaves on climbers and tall leaves up walls. With *No. 13* pipe pink flowers on climbers.

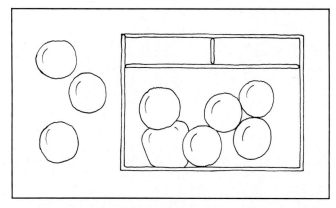

11. Brush underside and topside of the wedge with egg white, then position the roof. Colour some fondant flesh and some brown. Make 60 small balls and attach to the windows with egg white. Add the top half of a body to some – these should slope in at the bottom to show that the person is hanging out of the window.

12. Model six little bodies raising the roof, five can lean against the roof support to hide it, put one at the corner, as shown in the photograph. Model one more and position just peeping round the door. Secure all with egg white.

13. With *No. 1 nozzle* and dark brown, light brown and yellow icing, pipe hair on heads. Paint smiling lips and eyes. Carefully attach writing to silver board, using egg white and a line of icing to secure.

Passed driving test

This must rate as one of the happiest days in most people's lives. I think the immediacy of the result accounts for such overwhelming joy – being one of the few exams one takes where pass (or fail) is announced seconds after. I flung my arms round the examiner, kissed him profusely, dashed out of the car to tell my instructor and fell over a badly parked push-chair. Driving is now one of my favourite occupations.

The car is made from a 200mm (8in.) square cake. The ingredients and quantities for this are given on page 127 and method for baking on page 6–7. Instructions for making royal icing, marzipan and fondant are on page 7. The amount of fondant needed, 790g (1¾lb), is not large and so it can be made in one go; but remember to keep it securely wrapped in cling film until required.

The cake is not difficult to decorate and can be completed in one or two days, after the covering of marzipan has been left to dry for 48 hours.

Please read the General Notes on pages 6 to 9 before starting to decorate. Also read through the step-by-step instructions and check the ingredient and equipment lists.

Ingredients for fondant and royal icing

790g (1¾lb) icing sugar, plus 110g (4oz)
1¾ egg whites, plus ½
3½ tblsp liquid glucose
flavouring (optional)
Also: 560g (1¼lb) marzipan; warm sieved apricot jam; 50/50 mixture of cornflour and icing sugar in a dusting dredger; yellow, red, black, flesh, green and silver food colouring.

Equipment

Mixing bowls; spoons; sieve; rolling pin; steel rule; sharp-pointed knife; lolly sticks (LS) as spacers; pastry brush; small paint brush; greaseproof paper; Ateco (or equivalent) icing nozzles 1 and 2; 230mm (9in.) square silver cake board.

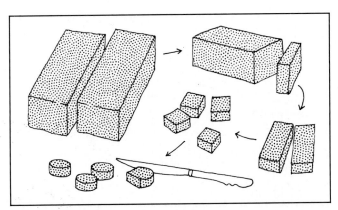

1. Slice the top of the cake flat, then cut in half. Cut a 25mm (1in.) slab from one half. Slice the slab in half, then cut each half in half again, as shown. Cut a wheel from each piece.

2. Round off the two large pieces of cake, as shown, then stick together with jam and a piece of marzipan.

Brush sides of cake with jam. Roll marzipan to 2 LS thick, lay cake on and cut round. Repeat with other side. Brush top, front and back with jam.

3. Cover with marzipan, in two pieces, as shown. Place the cake diagonally across the silver board. Roll the marzipan trimmings to 1 LS thick. Cover the edges and one side of each wheel.

Leave everything to dry for 48 hours.

4. Colour 450g (1lb) of fondant yellow. Cover the car as for marzipan, captions 2 and 3, using egg white instead of jam. Roll trimmings to 1 LS thick and cut four circles roughly 30mm (1¼in.) diameter. Cut a strip 2 LS thick to make a 55mm (2¼in.) circle, as shown.

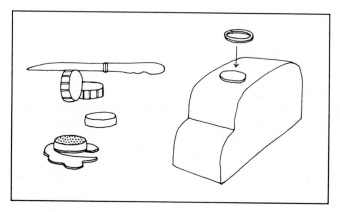

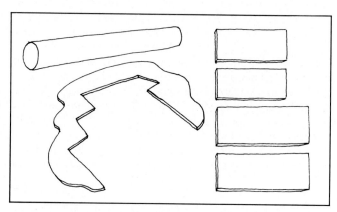

5. Take 110g (4oz) of fondant, colour black and roll to 1 LS thick. Cover wheels as for marzipan, caption 3, using egg white instead of jam. Mark tread with blunt edge of knife. Cut a black 55mm (2¼in.) circle and attach to car roof, towards the front. Stick strip of yellow around black circle.

6. Take 110g (4oz) of fondant, add some of the black fondant trimmings and partially mix to give a two-toned effect. Roll to 1 LS thick and cut four windows for sides, back and front of car, as shown.

7. Tilt the cake board backwards for easier application then attach windows with egg white. Trim the rounded corners of the side windows after application.

Make the 110g (4oz) of royal icing.

8. With *nozzle No. 2* and yellow icing, pipe two lines around the windows and down the centre of each (tip the board backwards). Pipe the door division and sill, door handle, radiator, windscreen wipers and the V above the radiator.

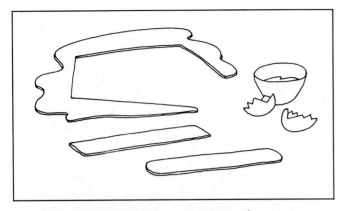

9. Roll some black fondant to 2 LS thick. Cut two bumper bars 12mm ($\frac{1}{2}$in.) deep. Round off the ends then attach to front and back of car with egg white.

10. Roll black trimmings to 1 LS thick. Cut four circles (lights) about 15mm ($\frac{5}{8}$in.) diameter. Apply to front and back of car, then paint the centres silver. Paint radiator, door handles and windscreen wipers.

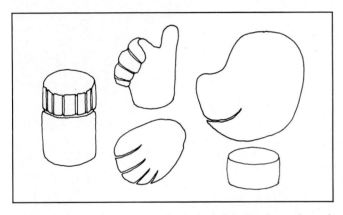

11. Colour some fondant flesh. Model head, neck and hands, as shown. Mark mouth and fingers with blunt edge of knife. Model the green arm, marking welt of jumper with knife. Leave to dry for one hour.

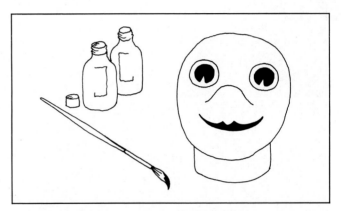

12. Make two flat circles from little white balls and attach to face, as shown. Paint eyes and lips. Carefully assemble and position body pieces, securing with egg white and icing, as if squeezing out of sun roof.

13. With *nozzle No. 1* pipe appropriate colour hair and eyebrows on figure. Roll a piece of white fondant to 1 LS thick. Cut to 35mm x 40mm (1$\frac{1}{4}$in. x 1$\frac{1}{2}$in.). Attach to hand and top of car with egg white, curling it, as shown.

14. Paint black printing and red ticks on the 'pass certificate' as shown.

Failed driving test

It would be a nice thought to prepare a surprise commiseratory party for the one who had just failed his/her driving test for the umpteenth time – but the person would need to have retained a smattering of humour, especially after so many failures. I had considered having a trail of flattened pedestrians, cats and possibly a point-duty policeman, laid out behind the car, but the idea, of course, is to have a laugh about the whole thing and encourage success next time.

The base is a 200mm (8in.) round cake. Ingredients and quantities for this are given on page 127 and the method for baking is on page 6–7. Instructions for making royal icing, marzipan and fondant are on page 7. If you are making your own fondant, it will be easier to make the 900g (2lb) in two batches, keeping them securely wrapped in cling film and in an airtight container until required.

The cake is not difficult to decorate and can be completed in a day, after the covering of marzipan has been left to dry for 48 hours. The most time-consuming part is painting the road signs.

Please read the General Notes on pages 6 to 9 before starting to decorate. Also read through the step-by-step instructions and check the ingredient and equipment lists.

Ingredients for fondant and royal icing

900g (2lb) icing sugar, plus 110g (4oz)
2 egg whites, plus $\frac{1}{2}$
4 tblsp liquid glucose
flavouring (optional)
Also: 450g (1lb) marzipan; warm sieved apricot jam; 50/50 mixture of cornflour and icing sugar in a dusting dredger; yellow, black, green, red, brown, lilac and flesh food colouring.

Equipment

Mixing bowls; spoons; sieve; rolling pin; steel rule; sharp-pointed knife; lolly sticks (LS) to use as spacers; pastry brush; small paint brush; greaseproof paper; Ateco (or equivalent) icing nozzles 1 and 3; 250mm (10in.) round silver cake board; thin card for templates.

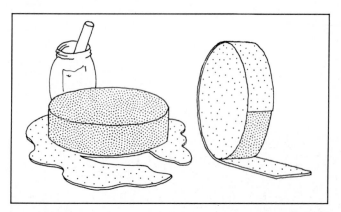

1. Slice the top of the cake flat, then brush with jam. Roll marzipan to 2 LS thick, lay cake on top and cut round the marzipan. Brush sides with jam. Roll marzipan to a long strip, then roll cake along, as shown. Leave to dry for 48 hours.

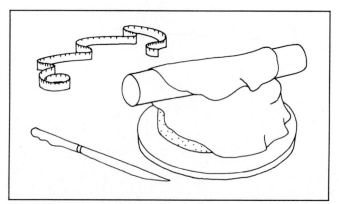

2. Position cake on silver board. Colour 560g (1¼lb) of fondant pale green. Roll to a circular shape, 2 LS thick and roughly 300mm (12in.) diameter. With help of rolling pin, carefully cover the cake. Trim round bottom edges.

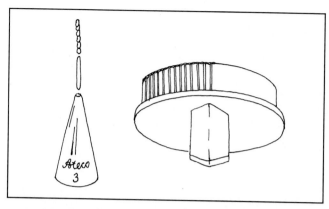

3. Make the 110g (4oz) of royal icing. With *No. 3 nozzle* and bright green icing, pipe vertical lines down sides of cake – tilt the board backwards so that the lines will adhere. Pipe continuous dots at top and bottom of lines.

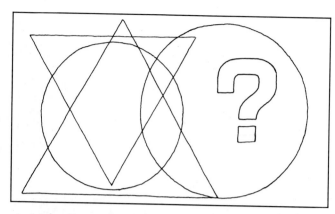

4. Make the card templates as shown above. Roll white fondant to 1 LS thick. Cut one 25mm (1in.) square. Cut eight small triangles and six small circles. Roll some red fondant to 1 LS thick and cut eight large triangles and six large circles. With *No. 1 nozzle* and red icing, pipe a question mark on the white square.

5. Add a little water to the red icing and fill in the question mark. Stick the white shapes on to the red ones, using egg white. Paint the signs black – as in the photograph.

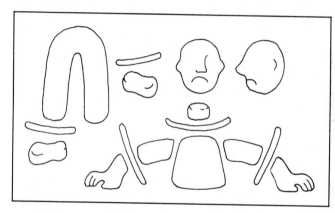

6. Colour pieces of fondant and model body parts, as shown (make yellow trousers, rather than the red ones shown on the photograph). Assemble parts with egg white. Position shoes on the cake first, then legs – bend a long roll in half. Position body. Attach arms, supporting with card until secure.

7. Position neck and head, then leave everything to dry overnight.
　Support question mark on legs. With *No. 1 nozzle* and brown icing, pipe hair (male or female), then a string around neck attached to square. Flatten small balls of white fondant and place in eye sockets.

8. Paint green eyes, red lips and black string.
　Roll fondant trimmings to 4 LS thick, cut into neat squares and use to support road signs. Position signs, using blobs of icing to secure.

House-warming

When someone has a house-warming party, it is usually given with a great sense of pride – they have moved into a property and decorated it in their own very special way. It has always amazed me how quickly, after moving, people feel happy to allow detailed inspection. We have lived in our present house for thirteen years and the experience has been not unlike painting the Forth Bridge, but we never manage to get back to the other end! Children, of course, always manage to find the piece of loose wallpaper and cannot resist pulling, they draw little things on perfectly secure wallpaper, they hide in wardrobes and loosen hinges, crack windows, chip paint. Perhaps we will have a house-warming when they have all left home.

The door, surround and step are made from a 300mm (12in.) square cake. Ingredients and quantities for this are given on page 127 and the method for baking on page 6–7. Instructions for making royal icing, marzipan and fondant are on page 7. If you make your own fondant it will be easier to make the 1.680kg (3¾lb) in several batches, keeping each piece securely wrapped in cling film and in an airtight container.

The cake will take one to two days to decorate, after the covering of marzipan has been left to dry for 48 hours.

Please read the General Notes on pages 6 to 9 before starting to decorate. Also read through the step-by-step instructions and check the ingredient and equipment lists.

Ingredients for fondant and royal icing

1.680kg (3¾lb) icing sugar, plus 170g (6oz)
3¾ egg whites, plus ¾
7½ tblsp liquid glucose
flavouring (optional)
Also: 1.570kg (3½lb) marzipan; warm sieved apricot jam; 50/50 mixture of cornflour and icing sugar in a dusting dredger; black, yellow, red, brown, green and gold food colouring.

Equipment

Mixing bowls; spoons; sieve; rolling pin; steel rule; sharp-pointed knife; lolly sticks (LS) as spacers; pastry brush; Ateco (or equivalent) icing nozzles 1, 2, 3, 4, 66 and 96; 330mm (13in.) square silver cake board.

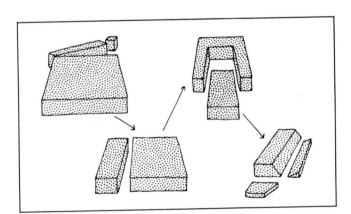

1. Slice the top of the cake flat. Cut a 25mm (1in.) piece from one side (this will be the bottom step) then cut 25mm (1in. from the end, as shown. Cut off a 100mm (4in.) slab (top step), then cut a door from remaining cake 100mm x 200mm (4in. x 8in.). Cut a 40mm (1½in.) slope from the door, as shown and 7mm (¼in.) from bottom.

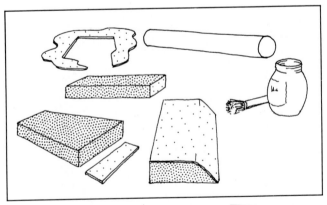

2. Roll marzipan to 2 LS thick. Brush sides of steps with jam. Cut marzipan to fit, then apply. Cover the steps (front and top of each with one piece) using the rolling pin to help with largest piece. Roll marzipan to 1 LS thick. Cover back of top step, back of door, back of surround, top and side of door.

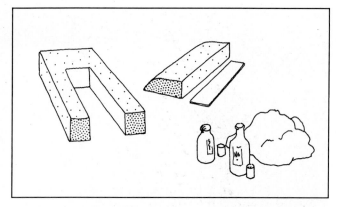

3. Roll marzipan to 2 LS thick. Cover sides, top and front of porch, then front of door. Leave everything to dry for 48 hours.

Colour 780g (1¾lb) of fondant grey. Cover steps, back of porch and back of door exactly as with marzipan but using egg white instead of jam.

4. Add 60g (2oz) of fondant to trimmings, then mix in yellow. Roll to 1 LS thick. Cover top and right-hand side of inside porch, then side of door. Secure large step (with blob of icing) 150mm (6in.) from front of board with small step in front.

Colour 560g (1¼lb) of fondant brick (red and black).

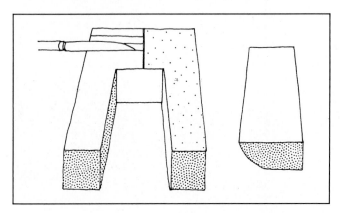

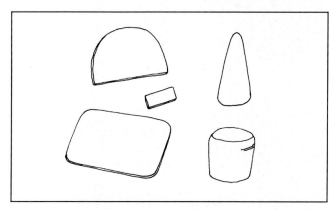

5. Roll fondant to 2 LS thick. Cut and apply pieces for sides, top and front (in two pieces) of porch, marking bricks with knife after each application. Colour 170g (6oz) of fondant the same colour as your own door. Roll to 2 LS thick, cut to size, and apply. Colour 60g (2oz) of fondant yellow. Roll to 1 LS thick.

6. Cut semi-circle to fit above door. Add brown to trimmings, cut door mat 70mm x 100mm (2¾in. x 4in.) and round off corners. Cut letterbox 10mm x 30mm (⅜in. x 1¼in.). Leave to dry on a dusted surface. Model a plant pot with brick trimmings. Add green to remaining trimmings and model a shrub.

7. With *No. 1 nozzle* and red icing, pipe **WELCOME** on door mat. Fill lettering in with dots, then pipe dark brown dots on remaining surface. With *No. 4* and dark brown icing, pipe trellis on right-hand side of wall. Attach semi-circle with egg white, then pipe around and mark windows. Pipe around door and down sides of opening. Pipe green ivy stems up left-hand side of wall. Pipe four rectangles on door (similar colour to door) then knocker and knob. With *No. 2* and darker green, pipe flower stems over trellis, needles on shrub and handle on letterbox. With lighter green, pipe stems on steps. With *No. 66* and dark and light green icing in the bag pipe the ivy leaves. With *No. 96* and white and pink icing in the bag, pipe flowers on trellis. With *No. 2* pipe yellow floor centres and flowers on steps. Position letterbox, door mat and plant pot with egg white. Carefully position porch (secure with icing) and slide door underneath. Cover top of door with fondant 1 LS thick. Paint letterbox, knocker and door knob with gold.

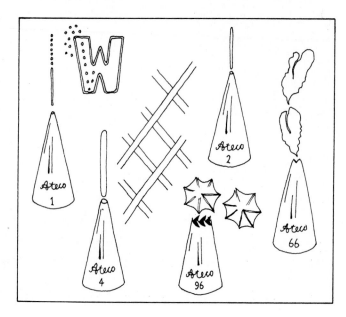

Office party

Christmas is usually the time for office parties, but there may be other reasons (or excuses) for revelry – the retirement of a staff member, centenary celebrations of the company, etc. As soon as my publisher saw this cake, she said, 'It suggests a debauch!' Which is true, but then some office parties tend to go that way! The success of the cake depends on how realistic the objects are, it helps to have the real thing in front of you while modelling. If you want to leave the objects on the tray loose, rather than securing them with icing, they can be given away as mementos at the end of the party.

The tray is made from two 200mm (8in.) square cakes. Ingredients and quantities for these are given on page 127 and the method for baking is on page 6–7. Instructions for making royal icing, marzipan and fondant are on page 7. If you are making your own fondant, it will be easier to make the 1.450kg (3$\frac{1}{4}$lb) in two or three batches, keeping it securely wrapped in cling film and in an airtight container until required.

The cake can be decorated in two days, after the covering of marzipan has been left to dry for 48 hours.

Please read the General Notes on pages 6 to 9 before starting to decorate. Also read through the step-by-step instructions and check the ingredient and equipment lists.

Ingredients for fondant and royal icing

1.450kg (3$\frac{1}{4}$lb) icing sugar, plus 60g (2oz)
3$\frac{1}{4}$ egg whites, plus $\frac{1}{4}$
6$\frac{1}{2}$ tblsp liquid glucose
flavouring (optional)
Also: 1kg (2$\frac{1}{4}$lb) marzipan; warm sieved apricot jam; 50/50 mixture of cornflour and icing sugar in a dusting dredger; red, green, yellow, black, gold and silver food colouring.

Equipment

Mixing bowls; spoons; sieve; rolling pin; steel rule; sharp-pointed knife; lolly sticks (LS) as spacers; pastry brush; small paint brush; greaseproof paper; Ateco (or equivalent) icing nozzle No. 3; two 250mm (10in.) square silver cake boards; cellotape; tin foil; waxed paper. To use as reference: bottle cork, ring pull and bottle cap.

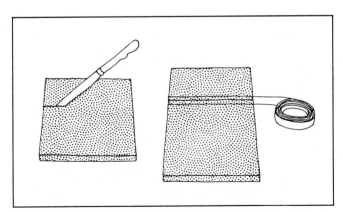

1. Cut one of the cake boards down to 100mm (4in.) then join it to the other with cellotape – the board will cut quite easily with a serrated bread knife. Cover the joined board neatly with tin foil.

2. Slice the tops of the cakes flat and cut one in half. Attach one of the halves, with jam and marzipan, to the whole cake. Cut the remaining half into four strips, as shown.

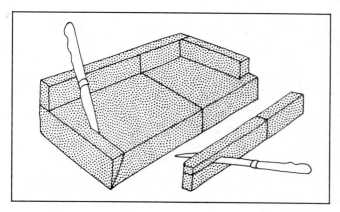

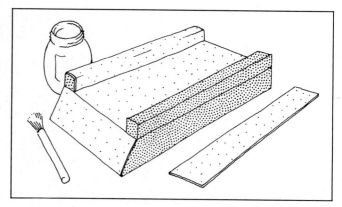

3. Cut the strips so they fit on three sides of the cake. Remove them and trim, so that they are not quite as deep as the cake.

Cut a slope from the main cake, as shown, then trim the ends of the two longest strips to fit.

4. Measure front, top and back of cake, then brush with jam. Roll marzipan to 2 LS thick, cut to fit and apply with the help of rolling pin. Trim edges. Attach longest strips of cake with jam, then cover insides and tops, as shown.

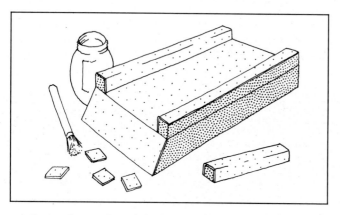

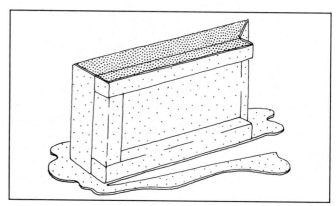

5. Cover three sides of the back strip of cake and position, securing with jam. Cut pieces of marzipan for both ends of the long strips of cake. Apply as before.

6. Carefully turn the cake on its side and cover, as shown. Repeat with the other side.

Leave the marzipan to dry for 48 hours.

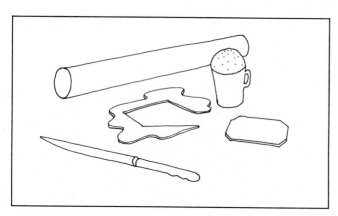

7. Meanwhile, take a little fondant, colour it green and roll to 1 LS thick. Cut a rectangle 45mm (1¾in.) deep and 90mm (3½in.) wide. Cut the corners off. Leave to dry on a dusted surface.

8. Colour 1kg (2¼lb) of fondant red. Cover the cake exactly as with marzipan, captions 4, 5 and 6, but using egg white instead of jam. Stand the cake on waxed paper when covering the last side.

Position the cake on the silver cake board.

IN TRAY

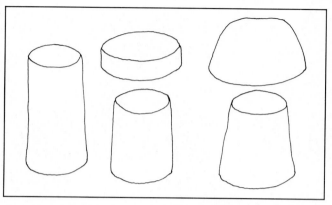

9. Make the 60g (2oz) of royal icing and colour red. Pipe a line of continuous dots along the outer edge seams of fondant. Pipe **IN TRAY** and two screw heads on the green plaque.

10. To make the corks, colour about 280g (10oz) of fondant with yellow, red and a little black — refer to a real cork. Model ten straight, four capped and two champagne, as shown. Leave to dry for three hours.

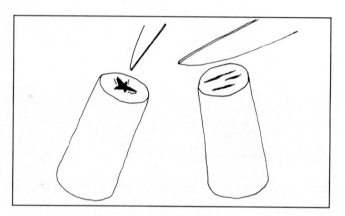

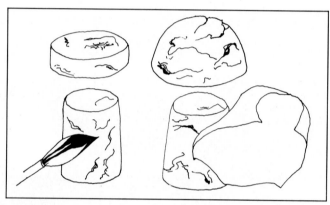

11. Pierce the tops of four straight corks with the pointed knife — to resemble hole made by cork screw. Mark irregular straight lines on tops of remaining straight corks, as shown.

12. Using black and a little red colouring, fill in the surface cracks on the champagne and capped corks — brush over the surface with colour, then wipe away excess with a slightly damp cloth. Leave the pieces to dry for an hour, then assemble with egg white.

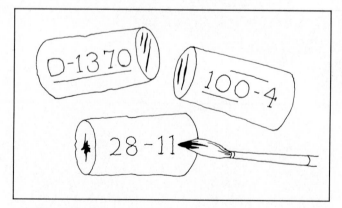

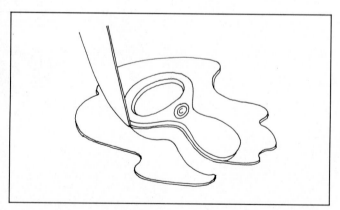

13. Paint straight corks lightly with black and a mixture of red, yellow and black. The result should not be as detailed as other corks. Fill in the irregular lines on the tops. Leave to dry, then paint numbers (with the mixed colour) on the sides of four corks, as shown.

14. Generously dust and knead some white fondant. Flatten a small piece with fingers, dust the working surface, lay the ring pull on the fondant and carefully cut round. Curl flap up slightly. Continue until seven have been made. Leave to dry.

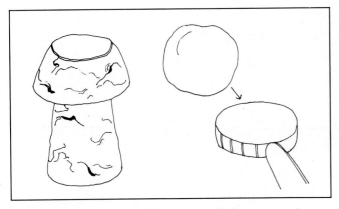

15. Flatten two circles of fondant with fingers, as shown, and attach to champagne corks with egg white. Roll remaining fondant into balls, roughly the size shown. Flatten into circles 6mm (just less than $\frac{1}{4}$in.) thick, then mark edges with round edge of a dinner knife.

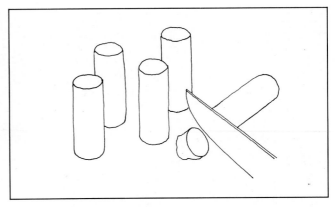

16. To make the cigarettes, colour some fondant with yellow, red and a little black – use a real cigarette for reference if possible. Make a perfectly smooth roll 25mm (1in.) long. Cut both ends straight. Make five in all.

17. Make five white rolls, exactly the same, but different lengths. Carefully stick white and brown rolls together with egg white. Leave to dry for about ten minutes. Using finger nails, pinch ends of cigarettes to make rough surface.

18. Paint a strong black line between rough and smooth surfaces, as shown. Using watered black, paint areas of the rough surface, leaving some white. Mix red, yellow and a little black, add water, then paint brown area coming away from the black line.

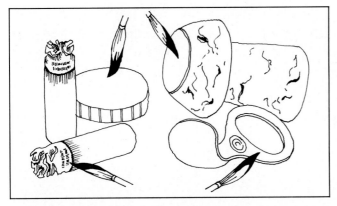

19. Paint three lines of fake lettering on white part of cigarettes, as shown. Paint the bottle tops gold. Paint the ring pulls, screw heads on plaque and tops of champagne corks, all silver.

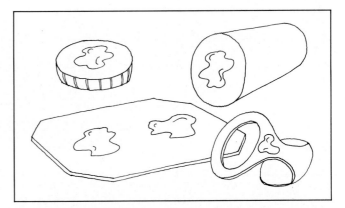

20. (Additional ring pulls and bottle tops can be made with red fondant trimmings, the colour will not show through the gold and silver).
Attach plaque to front of tray with dabs of icing. Position pieces in tray, leave loose, or secure with dabs of red icing.

Seven-year itch

The term *'seven-year itch'* is derived from the lease system – leases normally run in seven-year periods because of an ancient belief that during the 'climateric years' (7th, 14th, 21st, etc) life was especially prone to danger due to the malevolence of the presiding planet, Saturn. The obvious danger to a seven-year marriage is boredom, I suppose, itchy feet, a desire to look for greener pastures.

The couple in the cake apparently have no little itches in their seventh year. Romance is still very much in the air – but romance with whom? After the inevitable questions, I tried to explain to my children the significance of the two people behind the sofa, but eventually gave up, leaving them with my son's suggestion that the couple were intruders intent on pinching the wine!

The sofa and base are made from a 180mm (7in.) round cake and a 200mm (8in.) square cake. Ingredients for these are given on page 127 and method for baking on page 6–7. Instructions for making royal icing, marzipan and fondant are on page 7. If you make your own fondant it will be easier to make the 1.900kg (4¼lb) in several batches, keeping each piece securely wrapped in cling film and in an airtight container.

Please read the General Notes on pages 6 to 9 before starting to decorate. Also read the step-by-step instructions and check the ingredients and equipment lists.

Ingredients for fondant and royal icing
1.900kg (4¼lb) icing sugar, plus 110g (4oz)
4¼ egg whites, plus ½
8½ tblsp liquid glucose
flavouring (optional)
Also: 1.230kg (2¾lb) marzipan; warm sieved apricot jam; 50/50 mixture of cornflour and icing sugar in a dusting dredger; turquoise, lemon, red, green, black, orange, brown and silver food colouring.

Equipment
Mixing bowls; spoons; sieve; rolling pin; steel rule; sharp-pointed knife; lolly sticks (LS) to use as spacers; pastry brush; small paint brush; greaseproof paper; Ateco (or equivalent) icing nozzles 1, 2 and 3; 250mm (10in.) square silver cake board.

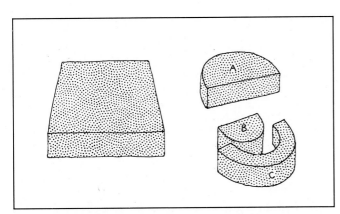

1. Slice the tops of the cakes flat. Cut the round cake in half, then cut a 115mm (4½in.) semi-circle from one half – **A B** and **C**.

Roll a piece of marzipan to 2 LS thick. Brush sides of square cake with jam. Lay each side on the marzipan and cut to fit.

2. Repeat with top of cake and the sides and top of **B**. To cover **C** measure the inside curve, brush with jam, cut marzipan to fit, then apply. Repeat with the back curve, front pieces and top.

Leave all the pieces to dry for 48 hours.

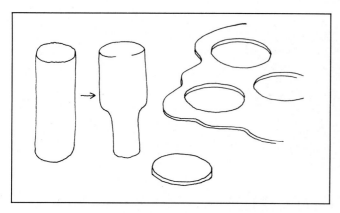

3. Roll about 15g (½oz) of fondant to 9mm (⅜in.) diameter. Cut the roll into four 25mm (1in.) pieces and model four goblets, as shown. Press trimmings flat and cut four 15mm (⅝in.) circles. Attach goblets to circles with egg white. Leave to dry on a dusted surface.

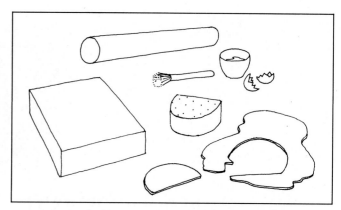

4. Colour 670g (1½lb) of fondant turquoise and cover the square cake exactly as for marzipan, but using egg white instead of jam.

   Mix 560g (1¼lb) of fondant with the blue trimmings and add lemon colour. Cover sides of **B**, then the top.

5. Cover inside curve and front of **C** (all at 2 LS thick), then front of **A**. Brush base of **C** with jam and attach to **A**. Cut a semi-circle to fit on seat area. Cut a piece to fit back, then carefully apply. Roll a piece roughly to shape of top, apply, then trim edges.

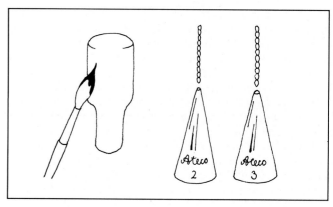

6. Paint sides of goblets silver. When dry, paint underneath. Paint tops with dark red (red mixed with a little black).

   Make the royal icing. With *No 2 nozzle* and turquoise icing pipe continuous dots along top fondant seam of square cake. With *No 3* pipe continuous dots round base.

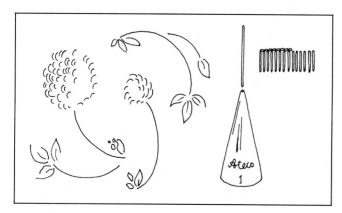

7. Paint red and green design on sofa and pouffe. With red icing and *No 1 nozzle*, pipe fringing around bottom of sofa and pouffe, then continuous dots along fondant seams. When dry, carefully secure to square cake with dabs of icing.

8. Add black to green trimmings. Break a piece off, add more black and model shoe, as shown. Make a roll with remainder, bend in half and secure to sofa and pouffe with egg white. Secure leg to shoe.

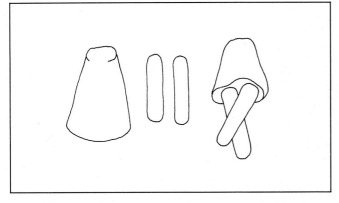

9. Colour 60g (2oz) of fondant turquoise, model the skirt as shown, then position it, securing with egg white. Colour 30g (1oz) of fondant with flesh colouring, model and position legs.

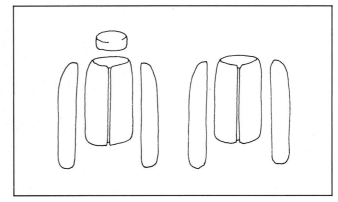

10. Colour 90g (3oz) of fondant orange, model and attach shoes. Colour 90g (3oz) brown and 150g (5oz) flesh. Make two bodies, four arms and a neck with orange and brown, as shown. Position orange body, neck and arms.

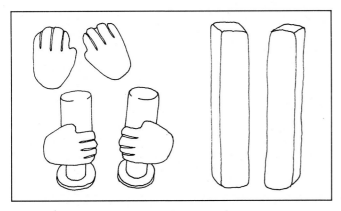

11. Secure brown body and arms. Model four hands, position two around two goblets, one on man's arm around woman and one on her arm resting on man's lap, then attach the two hands with goblets. Cut 90g (3oz) of fondant in half and make two square posts, same height as sofa. Attach to sofa back with egg white.

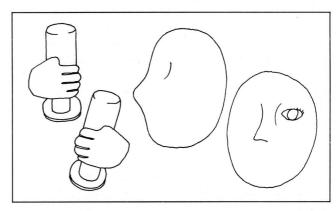

12. Make four heads and two hands with remaining flesh fondant. Attach hands to remaining goblets as before.
    Paint eyes on all faces, as shown, black moustache on gentleman friend and red lips on lady friend.

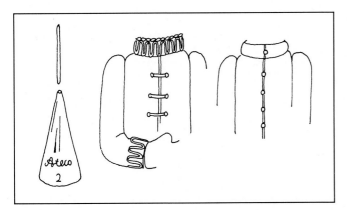

13. With *No 2 nozzle* and brown icing, pipe details on man's jacket, polo collar, welt on sleeves, fastenings and buttons down woman's jacket.

14. Attach heads to posts. *With No 2 nozzle* pipe blonde hair on lady friend, black hair on man friend and appropriate coloured hair on seated couple. Attach goblets to back of sofa, using a blob of icing to secure.

Get well

A little humour can be as therapeutic as any medicine and this cake should bring a wry smile to someone recovering from an illness or accident. I have been deliberately vague about the sexes of the patients, so you can copy the characters exactly, or be more specific and use the hair and eye colouring of your friend or relation.

The bed and bedside cabinets are made from a 200mm (8in.) square cake. Ingredients and quantities for this are given on page 127 and the method for baking on page 6–7. Instructions for making royal icing, marzipan and fondant are on page 7. If you make your own fondant it will be much easier to make the 1.570kg (3½lb) in three batches, keeping it securely wrapped in cling film and in an airtight container until required.

The cake will take one to two days to decorate, after the covering of marzipan has been left to dry for 48 hours. It needs to be cut into rather small pieces, in order to build the bedside cabinets, and bits of cake may come away while cutting. If this happens, try to stick them back, or fill the holes with marzipan. Do make sure you use a really sharp knife.

Please read the General Notes on pages 6 to 9 before starting to decorate. Also read through the step-by-step instructions and check the ingredient and equipment lists.

Ingredients for fondant and royal icing

1.570kg (3½lb) icing sugar, plus 60g (2oz)
3½ egg whites, plus ¼
7 tblsp liquid glucose
flavouring (optional)
Also: 900g (2lb) marzipan; warm sieved apricot jam; 50/50 mixture of cornflour and icing sugar in a dusting dredger; black, blue, yellow, red, green, flesh, brown and silver food colouring.

Equipment

Mixing bowls; sieve; spoons; rolling pin; steel rule; sharp-pointed knife; lolly sticks (LS) as spacers; pastry brush; small paint brush; greaseproof paper; Ateco (or equivalent) icing nozzles 1, 2 and 13; 350mm (14in.) square silver cake board.

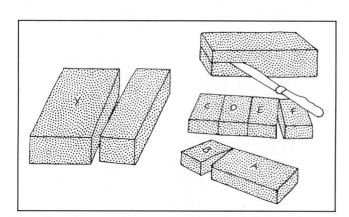

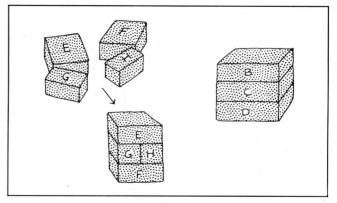

1. Slice the top of the cake flat. Cut from it a 75mm (3in.) slab, then slice this in half. Take one of the halves and cut off a 50mm (2in.) piece – the larger piece **A** will be positioned under the bed. Cut the other half into four 50mm (2in.) pieces – **C D E** and **F.**

2. Cut a 25mm (1in.) piece from **E** and **F.**
    Sandwich **B C** and **D** together with jam and a thin piece of marzipan. Repeat with **E F G** and **H**, as shown.

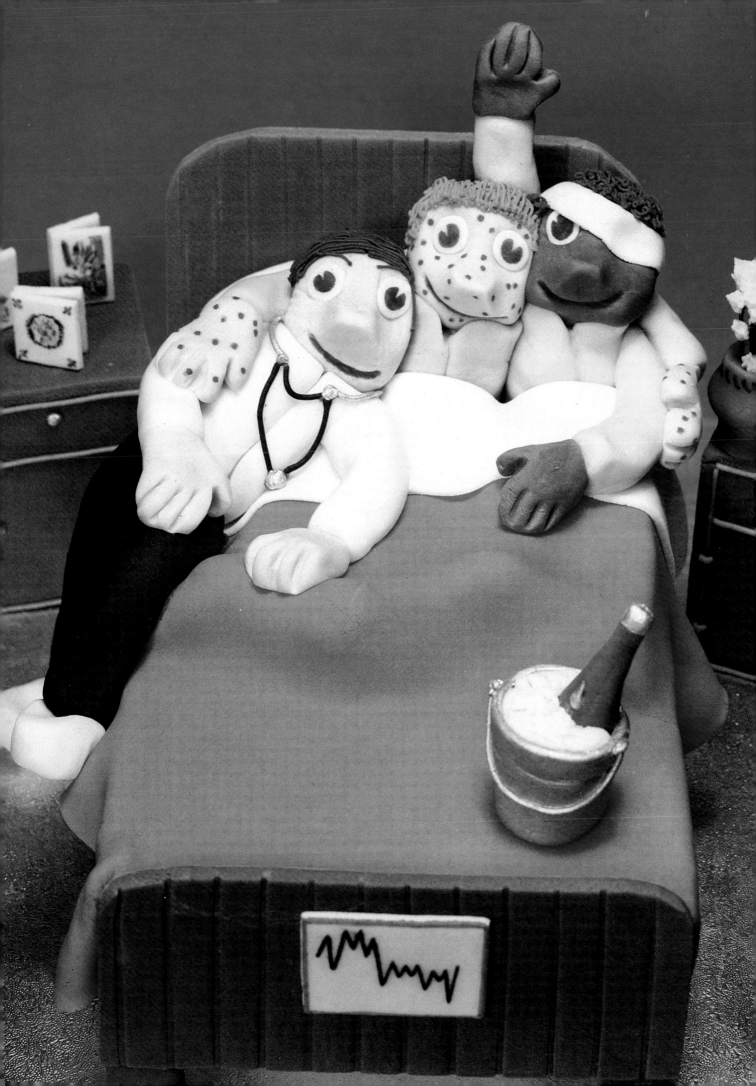

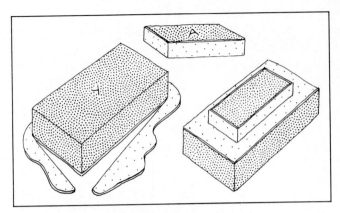

3. Roll marzipan to 1 LS thick. Brush **Y** (bed) underside with jam, lay on top of marzipan and cut round. Brush sides of base **(A)** and cover, still at 1 LS thick. Brush top of base with jam and stick in centre of bed underside.

4. Roll marzipan to 2 LS thick. Cover sides and top of bed, then the square and oblong blocks (bedside cabinets).
Leave everything to dry for 48 hours.

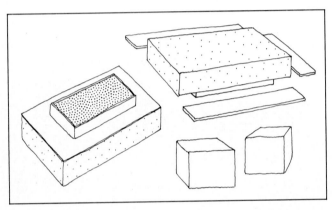

5. Take 560g (1¼lb) of fondant. Roll to 1 LS thick. After measuring, brush a thin film of egg white on base sides and bed underside. Cut fondant to fit, then apply.
Roll fondant to 2 LS thick and cover three sides of bed. Colour remaining fondant grey. Roll to 2 LS thick. Cover cabinets, sides first, then tops. Leave on one side.

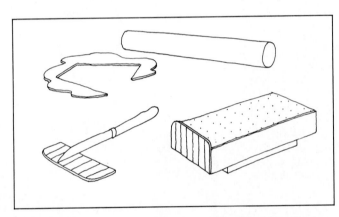

6. Roll fondant to 2 LS thick. Cut headboard 140mm x 70mm (5½in. x 2¾in.). Mark grooves with blunt edge of knife, round the top corners off, then leave on a dusted surface to dry. Cut base board 140mm x 60mm (5½in. x 2½in.), mark grooves, round off corners, then attach to bottom of bed with egg white.

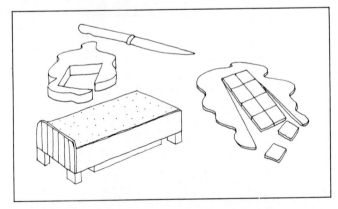

7. Position bed on the cake board, left of centre.
Roll remaining grey fondant to 4 LS thick. Cut four legs 20mm (¾in.) wide 25m (1in.) high. Brush the tops with egg white, then slide one under each corner of the bed. Roll a litle white fondant to 1 LS thick. Cut ten pieces about 20mm (¾in.) square.

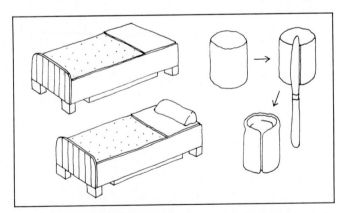

8. Take 110g (4oz) of white fondant. Roll to 1 LS thick, cut a piece 140mm x 60mm (5½in. x 2½in.) Attach to top end of bed. Model remaining fondant into a pillow, as shown, and position. Colour 110g (4oz) of fondant blue and 110g yellow. Use roughly half of each to model two bodies, as shown. Position on bed, securing with egg white.

74

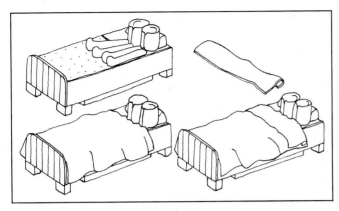

9. Take 100g (4oz) of white fondant, model four legs and position on bed. Take 220g (8oz) of fondant. Colour 170g (6oz) red, roll to 1 LS thick, roughly 270mm x 150mm (10½in. x 6in.). Carefully lift, and lay on bed. Roll remaining white to 1 LS thick 270m x 60mm (10½in. x 2½in.). Curl over and position at top edge of blanket.

10. Divide 100g (4oz) of fondant into three. Colour two portions flesh and one brown. Model the heads, as shown (leaving enough fondant to make hands), and position two. Take some white fondant, model and position doctor's body. Position head. Model all arms and position, securing with egg white.

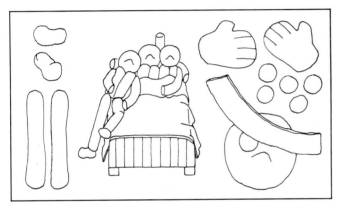

11. Model doctor's shoes, as shown. Take remaining fondant trimmings, add black. Model and position legs, securing with egg white. Model and position all the hands. Flatten with fingers five white round pieces and attach for eyes. Flatten a narrow strip and attach around one head.

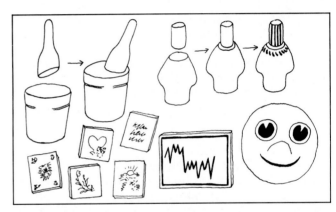

12. Model an ice bucket and bottle, as shown. Attach bottle, then roughen top surface of bucket with knife. Model a vase, attach a piece of green fondant as shown.

Paint eyes, lips and spots; temperature chart; dark green stalks and the pattern around vase; indications of design on five cards.

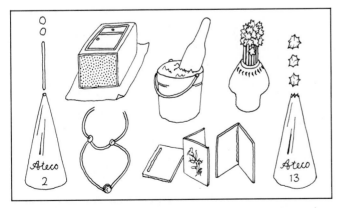

13. Put cabinets, on their backs, on waxed paper. With *No. 2 nozzle* pipe pale grey lines and knobs. Pipe handle on ice bucket, and stethoscope around doctor's neck. Pipe a small line at side (on inside) of each card and attach a back. With *No. 13 nozzle* pipe yellow daffodils on stalks.

14. Paint ice bucket, bottle top and cabinet knobs, silver. With *No. 1 nozzle* pipe appropriate coloured hair. Secure ice bucket to bed and temperature chart to base board with dabs of icing. Position cabinets. Secure vase with icing. Position cards then place a blob of icing at bottom of inside fold.

Novelty Birthday Cakes

Career woman

Although it has been socially acceptable for women to go out to work since the war, only now are careers for them expanding into previously male-dominated areas. More are taking high managerial posts and positions of authority and this cake, without being too specific, is for them.

The chair and desk are made from one 200mm (8in.) round cake and one 130mm (5in.) square cake. Ingredients and quantities for these are given on page 127 and method for baking on page 6–7. Instructions for making royal icing, marzipan and fondant are on page 7. If you make your own fondant it will be easier to make the 1.230kg (2¾lb) in three batches, keeping each piece securely wrapped in cling film and in an airtight container.

The cake will take one or two days to decorate, after the covering of marzipan has been left to dry for 48 hours.

Please read the General Notes on pages 6 to 9 before starting. Also read through the step-by-step instructions and check the ingredients and equipment lists.

Ingredients for fondant and royal icing

1.230kg (2¾lb) icing sugar, plus 110g (4oz)
2¾ egg whites, plus ½
5½ tblsp liquid glucose
flavouring (optional)
Also: 1kg (2¼lb) marzipan; warm sieved apricot jam; 50/50 mixture of cornflour and icing sugar in a dusting dredger; red; yellow, blue, brown, black and gold food colouring.

Equipment

Mixing bowls; spoons; sieve; rolling pin; steel rule; sharp-pointed knife; lolly sticks (LS) as spacers; pastry brush; small paint brush; greaseproof paper; Ateco (or equivalent) icing nozzles 1, 2, 3 and 65; 300mm (12in.) round silver cake board.

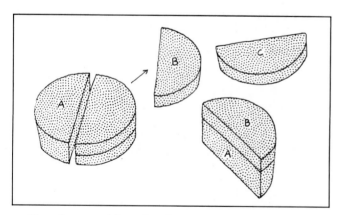

1. Slice the top of the cakes flat. Cut the round cake in half (**A**), then slice one of the halves in half (**B** and **C**). Attach **B** to **A** using jam on each surface and a sliver of marzipan in between.

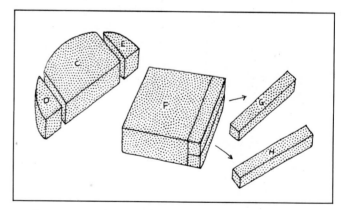

2. Cut 40mm (1½in.) from each side of **C**. Cut 25mm (1in.) from the square cake and slice it in half (**G** and **H**). Attach **C** to **F** using jam and marzipan as before.

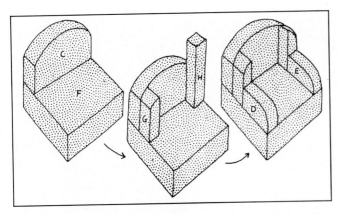

3. Put **G** and **H** against **C** and trim the ends to follow the curve, as shown. Put **D** and **E** against **G** and **F**, then cut the ends to fit flush with the chair front. Attach **D** to **G** and **E** to **H** using jam and marzipan as before.

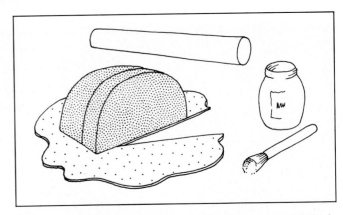

4. Brush back of desk with jam. Roll marzipan to 2 LS thick and apply as shown. Measure desk front, brush with jam, cut marzipan to fit, then apply. Brush top with jam, apply marzipan as for back.

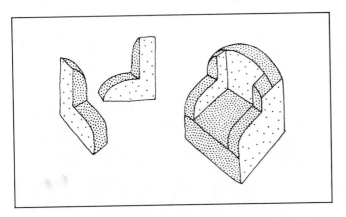

5. Roll marzipan to 1 LS thick and apply to inside of chair arms. Attach arms to chair with jam and a sliver of marzipan. Cover rest of chair (with marzipan at 2 LS thick) in the following order: inside back, back, and sides.

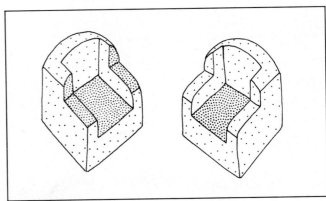

6. Continue with the front and arm fronts (in one piece), top and arm tops (in one piece), arm (in two pieces) and finally the seat.
   Leave the chair and desk to dry for 48 hours.

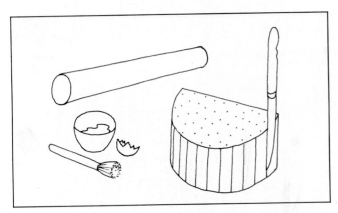

7. Follow instructions for applying marzipan, and cover desk (apart from top) and chair with fondant coloured with drops of yellow, red and blue. Apply with egg white instead of jam. After applying front of desk and inside back of chair, mark squares with blunt edge of knife.

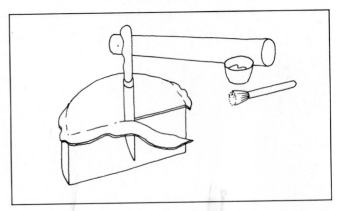

8. Add brown and black to trimmings, partially mix to give wood-grain effect. Roll to 2 LS thick and lay on table top (after brushing marzipan with a thin film of egg white). Trim the edges neatly.

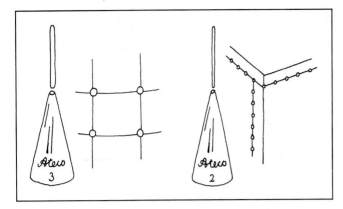

9. Make the royal icing. Colour some same colour as fondant. With *nozzle No 3* pipe buttons on upholstery. With *No 2* pipe nail heads on fondant seams of chair. When dry, paint gold.

Position both cakes on silver board, as shown.

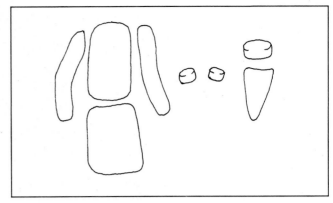

10. Colour 110g (4oz) of the fondant trimmings with black. Model body pieces as shown and secure in chair with egg white. Model white cuffs, collar and shirt front and attach with egg white. Colour about 45g ($\frac{1}{2}$oz) of fondant with flesh.

11. Model a knee and leg, as shown. Squeeze the knee between desk and chair with the leg next to it. Model head and hands, then attach. Model a little pink bow-tie, as shown, then attach. With *No 2* and appropriate coloured icing, pipe hair. Paint eyes and lips, then lace trim down front of shirt.

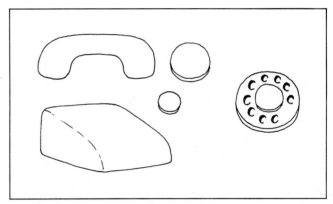

12. Mix the colours and model five telephones. Use just under 30g (1oz) for each. Cut the dials (white fondant) about 15mm ($\frac{5}{8}$in.) diameter and smaller circles (same colour as phones) for the centre of the dials. Attach receivers, dials and centres with egg white. Paint finger holes as shown.

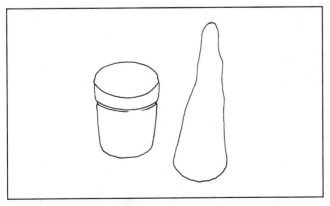

13. Colour a small piece of fondant with red and a little brown. Model a plant pot about 25mm (1in.) high. Mark a groove at top with blunt edge of knife. Model a green support, as shown, about 40mm (1$\frac{1}{2}$in.) high and attach to pot. Secure pot to corner of desk with a dab of icing.

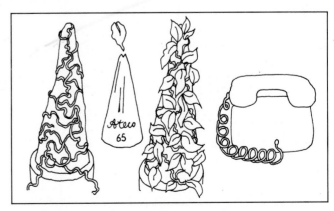

14. With *No 1 nozzle* and dark green icing, pipe squiggly stems over support, down side of pot, and on desk. With *No 65* and two shades of green in icing bag pipe variegated leaves. Secure telephones to desk with icing. With *No 2* and black icing, pipe curling leads from the handle to the back of each telephone.

Compulsive knitter

Hand-knitting was extremely popular in the late 1920s with designers like Elsa Schiaparelli producing knitwear to complement the lively, sporty fashion scene of the time: but, even through the 1950s (sloppy joes, Aran and mohair) and the stream-lined 1960s, clicking needles became synonymous with grannies and expectant mothers. In recent years, dyes and yarns have been developed and used in such exciting, imaginative ways that the art of hand-knitting has been given a new dimension. This cake, then, is for someone who knits compulsively, anywhere and any time.

The base is made from a 180mm (7in.) round cake. Ingredients and quantities for this are given on page 127 and the method for baking on page 6–7. Instructions for making royal icing, marzipan and fondant are on page 7.

The cake can be decorated in a day (after the covering of marzipan has been left to dry for 48 hours) but piping the balls of wool and the knitting around the sides of the cake is time-consuming, so you may find it easier to break off and finish the following day.

Please read the General Notes on pages 6 to 9 before starting to decorate the cake. Also read through the step-by-step instructions and check the ingredient and equipment lists.

Ingredients for fondant and royal icing

560g (1¼lb) icing sugar, plus 280g (10oz)
1¼ egg whites, plus 1¼
2½ tblsp liquid glucose
flavouring (optional)
Also: 450g (1lb) marzipan; warm sieved apricot jam; 50/50 mixture of cornflour and icing sugar in a dusting dredger; orange, green, red, yellow, blue and gold food colouring.

Equipment

Mixing bowls; spoons; sieve; rolling pin; steel rule; sharp-pointed knife; lolly sticks (LS) as spacers; pastry brush; small paint brush; greaseproof paper; Ateco (or equivalent) icing models 1 and 3; waxed paper; adhesive tape; stiff card; 230mm (9in.) round silver cake board.

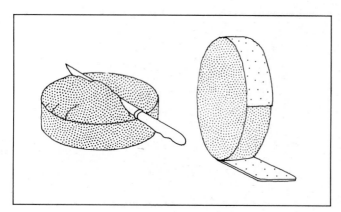

1. Slice the top of the cake flat, then turn over. Roll marzipan to 2 LS thick and cut a strip to the same depth and circumference as the cake. Brush cake sides with jam, then roll it along the strip, as shown.

2. Brush the top of the cake with jam. Roll marzipan to 2 LS thick and place cake on top. Neatly cut round.
   Leave the cake to dry for 48 hours.

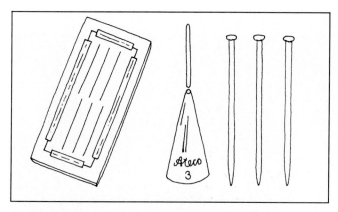

3. Meanwhile make the royal icing. Draw several lines, 60mm (2½in.) long, on the stiff card. Tape waxed paper over the card. Using *No. 3 nozzle*, pipe the lines, dragging the nozzle at the end so as to finish with a point. Pipe a dot at the beginning of each line, as shown. Leave to dry.

4. Take about 45g (1½oz) of fondant and model a support for the knitting, as shown. Take 75g (2½oz) of fondant, divide into five and colour with red, blue, green, yellow and orange. Make two balls from each colour, then cut each ball in half. Leave on a dusted surface.

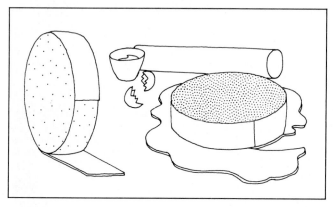

5. Cover the cake with white fondant, exactly as for marzipan but using egg white instead of jam. Position the cake on the silver board.

Paint the needles, while they are still attached to the waxed paper, with gold.

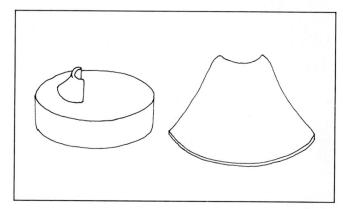

6. Secure the support to the cake with a dab of icing. Roll fondant to 1 LS thick and cut out the knitting shape, as shown – it will drape from the support to the edge of the cake.

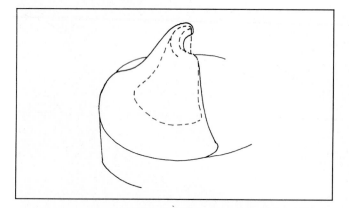

7. Fix the shape to the support with egg white – attach it about one quarter of the way down the back of the support, then over the top and out towards the edges of the cake. Smooth the edge so that it blends into the cake fondant.

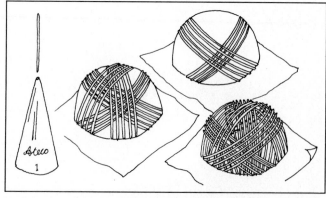

8. Put each half-ball on to a little square of waxed paper. Colour two to three teaspoons of icing with blue. Using *nozzle No. 1* pipe lines of wool over four of the half-balls, as shown. Leave to dry for about 20 minutes.

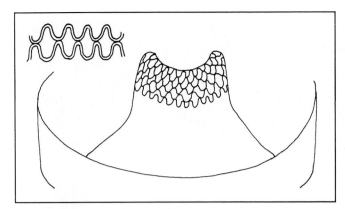

9. Starting at the top of the support, pipe six rows of knitting as shown. When the band is complete, pipe a loopy line down each side to neaten the edge.

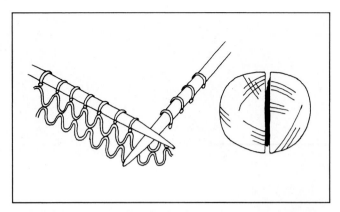

10. Choose the best pair of knitting needles. Carefully remove tape from waxed paper and card, then peel waxed paper from back of needles. Neatly secure on the first row of knitting with tiny lines of icing. Carefully pipe stitches over the needles. Join blue half-balls together with blob of icing.

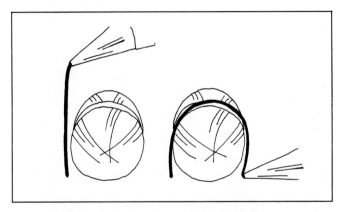

11. Stand the two balls on waxed paper. Pipe lines all the way around to cover up the join – hold nozzle just above the back of the ball, allow icing to fall, then move nozzle around to the front, tucking the line of icing underneath. Quickly push hanging line at the back underneath, using finger nail or knife point.

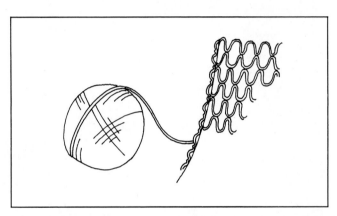

12. Leave the balls to dry for 20 minutes, then carefully position them on the cake (as shown in photograph) with a neat blob of icing. Pipe a strand of wool coming from each – the one in the foreground going behind the piece of knitting and up to the needles.

13. Repeat captions 7 to 9, using red icing. Position the balls as shown in the photograph, then pipe a strand of wool coming from each.

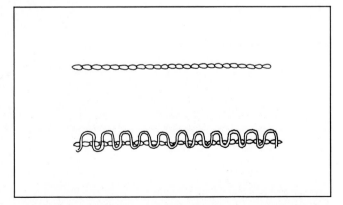

14. Continue until all the balls and knitting around the sides of the cake are complete. Pipe a continuous row of dots, in red, around the bottom edge of the cake, then pipe a row of loops over it.

Harassed mother

Last summer my eleven-year-old took the car keys and reversed our estate car into a telegraph pole. He then demolished our neighbour's gate, fence and Rhododendron bushes. When asked why, he said the car had been very carelessly parked and he was trying to straighten it up!

Having just bound and gagged her three children (and teddy bear), the harassed mother on this cake – feet immersed in warm water and reading a good book – is snatching a few precious moments of peaceful silence.

The base is made from a 200mm (8in.) square cake. Ingredients and quantities for this are given on page 127 and method for baking on page 6–7. Instructions for making royal icing, marzipan and fondant are given on page 7. If you are making your own fondant, you may find it easier to make the 1kg (2¼lb) in two batches, keeping each piece securely wrapped in cling film and in an airtight container until required.

The cake can be decorated in a day, after the covering of marzipan has been left to dry for 48 hours.

Please read the General Notes on pages 6 to 9 before starting to decorate. Also read through the step-by-step instructions and check the ingredients and equipment lists.

Ingredients for fondant and royal icing

1kg (2¼lb) icing sugar, plus 60g (2oz)
2¼ egg whites, plus ¼
4½ tblsp liquid glucose
flavouring (optional)
Also: 780g (1¾lb) marzipan; warm sieved apricot jam; 50/50 mixture of cornflour and icing sugar in a dusting dredger; green; blue; flesh, red, yellow and brown food colouring.

Equipment

Mixing bowls; spoons; sieve; rolling pin; steel rule; sharp-pointed knife; lolly sticks (LS) as spacers; pastry brush; small paint brush; greaseproof paper; Ateco (or equivalent) icing nozzles 1 and 2; 250mm (10in.) square silver cake board.

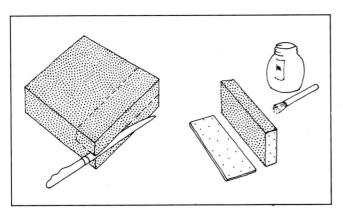

1. Slice the top of the cake flat. Carefully slice a 70mm (2¾in.) piece from the cake, as shown. Roll marzipan to 2 LS thick. Brush the sides of the piece with jam, cut the marzipan to fit, then apply. Repeat with front, then top.

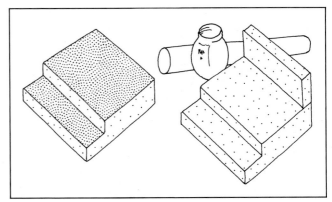

2. With marzipan still at 2 LS thick, cover the cake sides, then step fronts, then step tops. Brush the underside of the piece with jam and attach to the cake, as shown. Measure the back, brush with jam, cut marzipan to fit, then apply. Leave to dry for 48 hours.

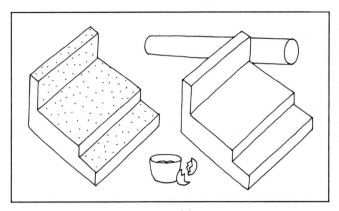

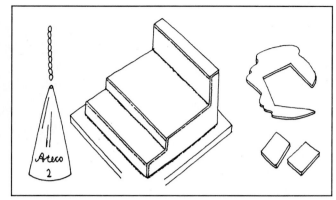

3. Colour 780g (1¾lb) of fondant pale green. Cover the cake with pieces at 2 LS thick in the following order: back, sides, front of steps, front of back, top of back, top of steps – brush marzipan surface with a thin film of egg white before applying fondant. Carefully position cake on cake board.

4. Make the royal icing. With *No 2 nozzle* and pale green icing, pipe continuous dots along all the fondant seams.

Break off a little white fondant and roll to 1 LS thick. Cut two pieces 20mm x 25mm (¾in. x 1in.). Leave on a dusted surface to dry.

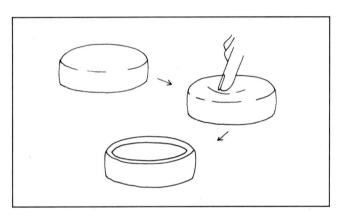

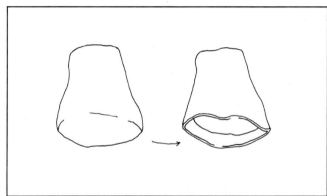

5. Break off 30g (1oz) of green fondant trimmings. Add more green colouring and model a basin – make a flat circle, indent the top with finger, then turn over and swivel round so that the basin rim becomes level. Carefully attach to bottom step with egg white.

6. Take another 60g (2oz) of fondant trimmings and add blue colouring. Using half, model the skirt, nipping out the base to give the appearance of fabric. Position with egg white on the step above the basin.

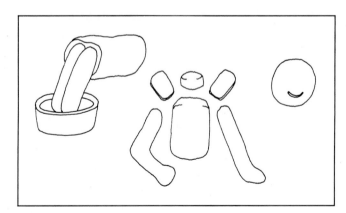

7. Colour 90g (3oz) of fondant with flesh colouring. Break off a piece, model the legs, and attach to skirt and basin, as shown. Model and attach body, arms, sleeves, and neck. Model head, mark smiling mouth with knife point, then attach to neck.

8. Use the remaining flesh fondant to make two pairs of legs and four heads, as shown. Colour a small piece of fondant brown. Roll, then flatten, and attach around faces, as shown.

Paint eyes on mother and children. Paint the design and lettering on book cover.

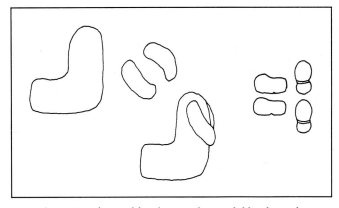

9. Colour 15g (½oz) of fondant pink. Model body and arms, as shown. Attach arms going round back. Attach to cake, then attach legs and head. Model small dark pink shoes, mark a line between sole and heel with blunt edge of knife. Attach the shoes.

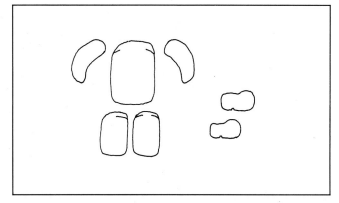

10. Colour just under 30g (1oz) of fondant orange. Model shorts, body and arms, as shown. Position, securing with egg white. Attach head and legs. Model little brown shoes, as before, then attach.

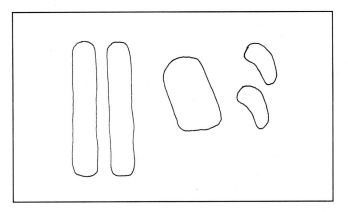

11. Colour 30g (1oz) of fondant blue. Model legs and attach to cake. Colour just under 30g (1oz) of fondant red. Model body and arms as shown, then attach to legs – body leaning forward slightly.

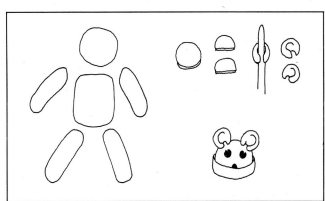

12. Attach head. Model black shoes and attach. Colour 30g (1oz) of fondant pale brown. Model teddy pieces as shown. Flatten a small piece for the ears, cut in half, then curl each piece around paint brush handle. Paint eyes and nose. Attach a dark brown gag. Assemble parts and attach to bottom step.

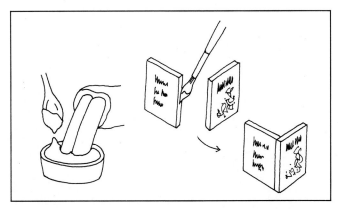

13. Add water to half a teaspoon of white icing. Pour the mixture into the fondant basin.

　　Brush some icing along the edge of half of the book cover, then join it to the other, as shown. Leave to dry.

14. With *No 1 nozzle* and appropriate coloured icing, pipe hair on mother and children. Carefully position book on mother's lap – pipe two blobs of icing to secure.

Diet freak

This is for those (and I am one) who are excessively weight conscious, the life-long dieter: we seldom achieve our elusive 'ideal weight' and if we do, we immediately relax, indulge again and are back to square one. We are the ones who sigh, 'Blessed are those who eat fat and remain thin.'

The cake could be presented as a birthday cake, or given at the end of a successful (or failed) diet.

The base is a 200mm (8in.) square cake. Ingredients and quantities for this are given on page 127 and the method for baking is on page 6–7. Instructions for making royal icing, marzipan and fondant are given on page 7. If you are making your own fondant, it will be easier to make the 900g (2lb) in two batches, keeping it securely wrapped in cling film and in an air-tight container, until required.

Gum tragacanth, which can be bought from most chemists, is used as a hardening agent for the plate. The cake is very simple to decorate (the striped effect may take a little time, but it is not difficult) and can be completed in one to two days, after the plate and covering of marzipan have been left to dry for 48 hours.

Please read the General Notes on pages 6 to 9 before starting to decorate. Also, read the step-by-step instructions, and check the ingredient and equipment lists.

Ingredients for fondant and royal icing

900g (2lb) icing sugar, plus 60g (2oz)
2 egg whites, plus $\frac{1}{4}$
4 tblsp liquid glucose
1 teasp gum tragacanth
flavouring (optional)
Also: 670g ($1\frac{1}{2}$lb) marzipan; warm sieved apricot jam; 50/50 mixture of cornflour and icing sugar in a dusting dredger; blue, yellow, bright green, and silver food colouring.

Equipment

Mixing bowls; spoons; sieve; rolling pin; steel rule; sharp-pointed knife; lolly sticks (LS) as spacers; pastry brush; small paint brush; greaseproof paper; Ateco (or equivalent) icing nozzles 1, 2 and 3; 250mm (10in.) square silver cake board; waxed paper; 180mm (7in.) round plate.

1. Cut a 180mm (7in.) circle of waxed paper. Make 30mm ($1\frac{1}{4}$in.) cuts around the edge and position it on the plate. Dust liberally.

2. Mix the teaspoon of gum tragacanth with a little water. Take 170g (6oz) of fondant, add the liquid gum, and dust liberally while kneading. Add drops of blue colouring. Knead well, then roll to 2 LS thick.

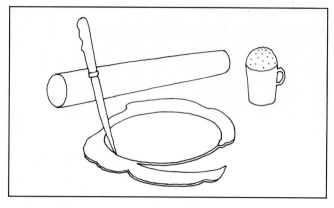

3. Cut a 180mm (7in.) circle – cut round a baking tin if possible. Carefully lift and position on the plate. Smooth the fondant with fingers. Leave to dry.

4. Cut the top of the cake flat, then turn over. Brush the sides with jam. Roll marzipan to 2 LS thick. Lay each side of the cake on the marzipan and cut to fit. Repeat this process for the top.

Leave the cake and plate to dry for 48 hours.

5. Take 670g (1½lb) of fondant and colour half yellow. Dust a sheet of waxed paper. Roll thin pieces of fondant, approximately 240mm (9½in.) long. Push them gently together, yellow and white alternately, using a little egg white if they do not adhere. Continue until a 240mm (9½in.) square is complete.

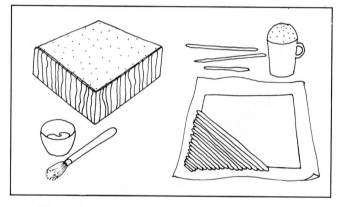

6. Roll the square to 2 LS thick. Measure the cake depth, then cut a piece to fit each side. Apply with egg white. Trim edges.

Draw cake size, with a strong black line, on a piece of waxed paper. Turn it over and dust. Repeat caption 5, taking the strips diagonally across.

7. When the square is complete, roll to 2 LS thick. Carefully (but confidently) flip the square over on to another sheet of waxed paper. Lightly brush the cake top with egg white.

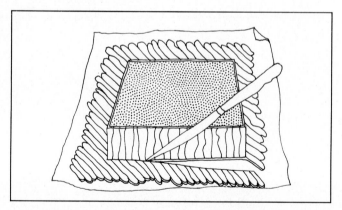

8. Carefully lay the cake on the fondant, then trim the edges. Lift the cake, position in the silver board and smooth the fondant surface with hands.

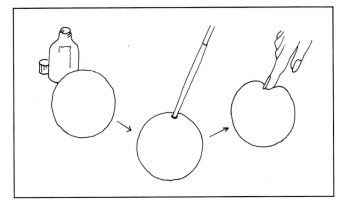

9. Take some of the fondant trimmings, add red, and roll into a very smooth ball. Indent the top centre with paint brush handle and then with index finger. Place carefully on a dusted surface and leave to dry.

10. Colour a small piece of fondant dark green — add a little red to yellow and blue. Roll the stalk as shown and bend it slightly. Press remaining fondant until fairly thin, then cut calyx. Gently ease calyx into tomato. Push paint brush handle down centre and position the stalk in the hole.

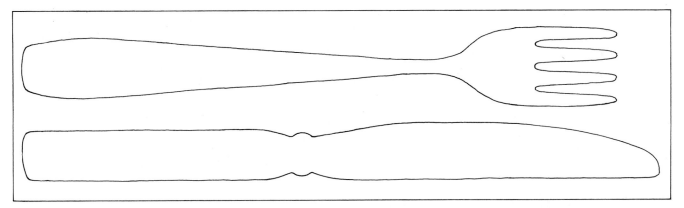

11. Make the 60g (2oz) of royal icing.

   Trace the above drawings on to greaseproof paper. Attach each drawing to the cake with a tiny dab of icing. Using a sewing needle, prick through the pencil lines into the fondant.

12. With *No. 2 nozzle* pipe white icing over the needle marks. Leave to dry for an hour, then add drops of water to some of the icing. Using a small spoon, carefully fill in the outlines. Leave to dry for 2–3 hours, longer if possible.

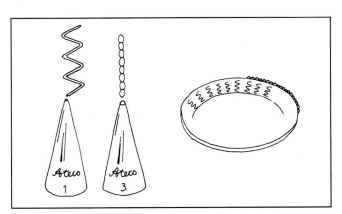

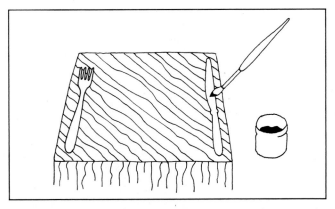

13. Carefully slide fondant plate from waxed paper and plate. With *No. 1 nozzle* pipe swiggles on plate, as shown. Add a drop of blue to remaining icing, and with *No. 3* pipe continuous dots round plate edge.

14. Paint knife and fork with silver. Secure plate on cake with a dab of icing. Carefully transfer tomato to plate, taking care not to squash, or the surface will crack. Secure with a dab of icing.

Computer maniac

Computers appear to have become an integral part of our lives: children are instructed in them at school, and classes are available which teach the use of computers in household accountancy, or enable mothers to keep pace with the technology until returning to work.

There are those who feel threatened by computers, those who are indifferent, and those who are obsessed by them – this cake is for the latter!

The computer is made from one 180mm (7in.) square cake and one 230mm (9in.) square cake. Ingredients and quantities for these are given on page 127 and the method for baking on page 6–7. Instructions for making royal icing, marzipan and fondant are on page 7. If you make your own fondant you may find it easier to make the 1.340kg (3lb) in two of three batches, keeping each piece securely wrapped in cling film and in an airtight container until required.

The cake can be decorated in one to two days, after the covering of marzipan has been left to dry for 48 hours. The design on the screen – a birthday cake firing and being fired at – can easily be changed to something more appropriate or personal. Just follow the basic instructions using your own drawings or lettering.

Please read the General Notes on pages 6 to 9 before starting to decorate. Also read through the step-by-step instructions and check the ingredients and equipment lists.

Ingredients for fondant and royal icing

1.340kg (3lb) icing sugar, plus 110g (4oz)
3 egg whites, plus $\frac{1}{2}$
6 tblsp liquid glucose
flavouring (optional)
Also: 1.120kg (2$\frac{1}{2}$lb) marzipan; warm sieved apricot jam; 50/50 mixture of cornflour and icing sugar in a dusting dredger; yellow, brown, black, green, blue and red food colouring.

Equipment

Mixing bowl; spoons; sieve; rolling pin; steel rule; sharp-pointed knife; lolly sticks (LS) as spacers; pastry brush; greaseproof paper; Ateco (or equivalent) icing nozzles 1 and 2; tracing paper; waxed paper; stiff white card; cellotape; 280mm (11in.) square silver cake board.

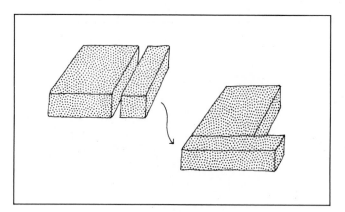

1. Slice the tops of both cakes flat. Cut a 50mm (2in.) slab from the smaller cake; attach it to one of the narrow sides using jam and a sliver of marzipan. Trim excess cake to give a 230mm x 130mm (9in. x 5in.) oblong.

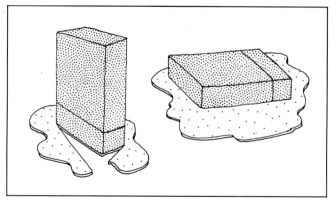

2. Roll marzipan to 2 LS thick, brush narrow ends of narrow cake with jam. Stand cake on marzipan and cut around, as shown. Brush top and front with jam. Roll marzipan to 2 LS thick. Lay cake on as before, covering top and front with one piece.

3. Cover three sides and top of square cake, as with narrow cake. Roll marzipan to 1 LS thick and cover underside of cake (which will be the back when it stands up).

Leave both cakes to dry (square cake standing on uncovered side) for 48 hours.

4. Colour 1.120kg (2½lb) of fondant yellow with a little brown. Knead well. Cover both cakes exactly as for marzipan, but using egg white to secure instead of jam.

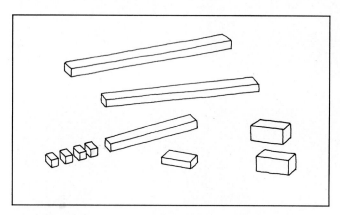

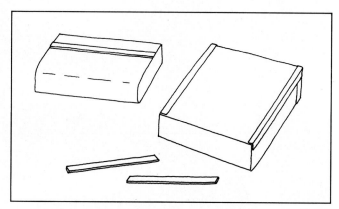

5. Add 220g (8oz) of fondant to trimmings, then mix in brown. Roll to 4 LS thick. Cut strips 13mm (½in.) wide. Cut strips into 49 cubes. Smooth the top edges of each with fingers. Cut one strip 120mm (4¾in.), two strips 30mm (1¼in.) and two 25mm (1in.) long. Roll fondant to 6 LS thick and cut two strips 40mm (1½in.) and one 30mm (1¼in.)

6. Roll fondant to 1 LS thick, cut a narrow strip and attach to keyboard with egg white. Leave all other pieces on lightly dusted surface. Roll fondant to 1 LS thick. Cut ten pieces 10mm (⅜in.) wide for front and top of square cake. Attach with egg white. Apply to side and top first, then front, then top corners.

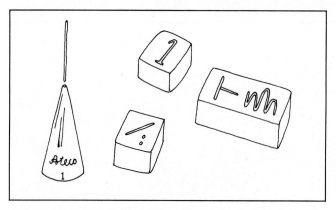

7. Make the royal icing. Take two or three teaspoonsful and colour with yellow and a little brown. With *nozzle No 1* pipe letters, numbers and symbols on pieces, as shown in photograph. Neatly secure each piece in position with a dab of icing.

8. Break off half remaining brown fondant and add a little black. Roll to 1 LS thick and cut a piece 140mm x 165mm (5½ x 6½in.). Round off the corners. Lay square cake on its back. Brush a thin film of egg white on area to be covered, then carefully apply piece.

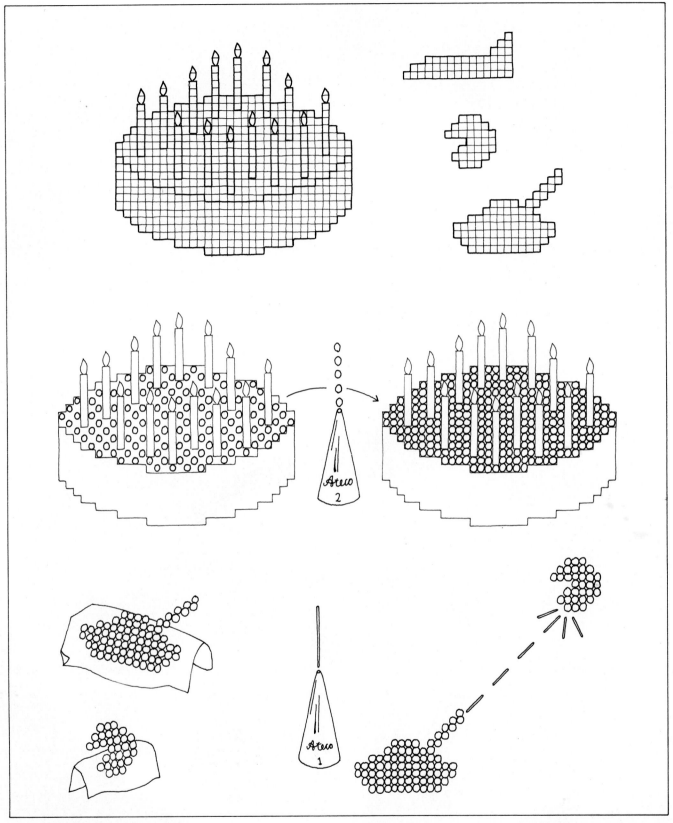

9. Trace the above drawings on to stiff white card. Tape waxed paper over the drawings then, using fairly stiff icing and *No 2 nozzle*, pipe a dot in each square (the dots must touch but not run into each other) – pipe the area with alternate dots, leave for 30 minutes, then fill in the remaining dots, as shown.

10. Use white for birthday cake top and candle flames; pale grey for cake front, blue candles, red tanks, yellow pac-men and green planes. Leave to dry overnight.

Carefully remove wax paper and attach pieces to screen with dark icing. With *No 1* pipe white fire marks. Attach cake to keyboard with blobs of icing.

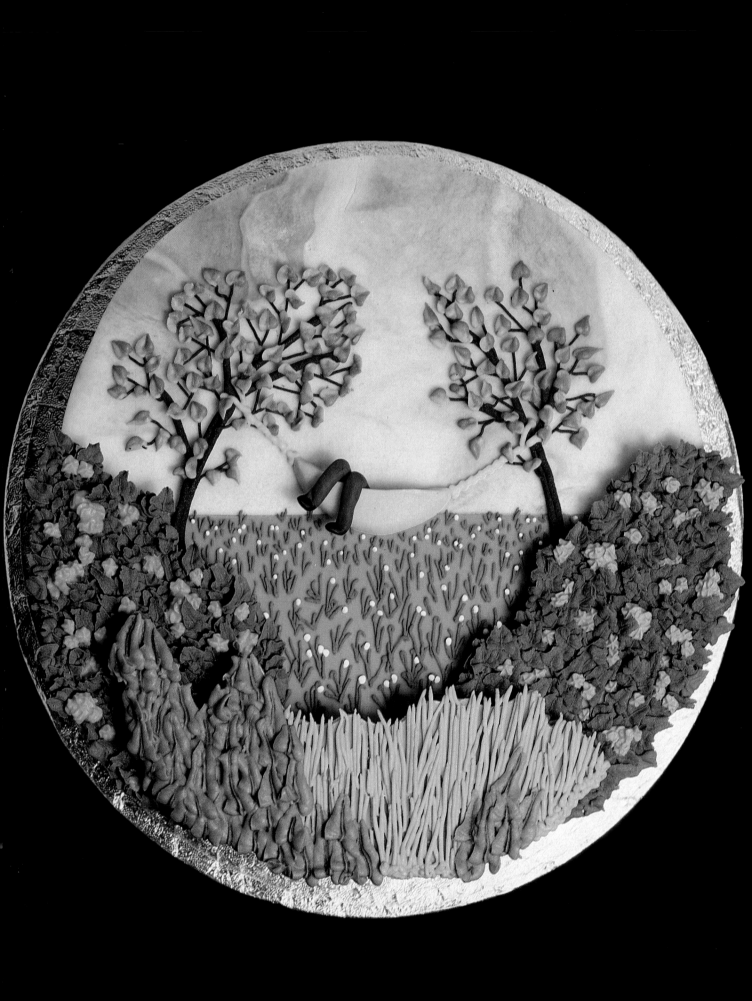

Lazy gardener

There are those for whom weeding, mowing lawns, sewing seeds, planting bulbs and trimming hedges is a labour of love. And there are those into whom these tasks strike terror. This gardener has finally succumbed to his nagging family and made an effort to explore unknown terrain – only to put up a hammock and experience the pleasure of sleep in the open air.

The base is made from a 200mm (8in.) round cake. Ingredients and quantities for this are given on page 127 and method for baking on page 6–7. Instructions for making royal icing, marzipan and fondant are given on page 7. If you are making your own fondant, keep it securely wrapped in cling film and in and airtight container until required.

The cake can be decorated in a day (after the covering of marzipan has been left to dry for 48 hours) but in order to allow the pieces of foreground to dry properly, it is best to leave them for one night and assemble everything the following day.

Please read the General Notes on pages 6 to 9 before starting to decorate. Also read through the step-by-step instructions and check the ingredient and equipment lists.

Ingredients for fondant and royal icing

560g (1¼lb) icing sugar, plus 280g (10oz)
1¼ egg whites, plus 1¼
2½ tblsp liquid glucose
flavouring (optional)
Also: 450g (1lb) marzipan; warm sieved apricot jam; 50/50 mixture of cornflour and icing sugar in a dusting dredger; yellow, green, blue, red, brown and black food colouring.

Equipment

Mixing bowls; spoons; sieve; rolling pin; steel rule; sharp-pointed knife; lolly sticks (LS) to use as spacers; pastry brush; small paint brush; greaseproof paper; Ateco (or equivalent) icing nozzles 1, 2, 3, 13, 65 and 66; 250mm (10in.) round silver cake board.

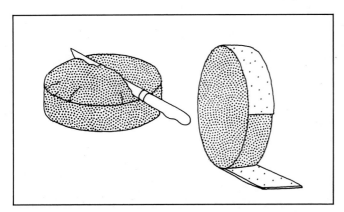

1. Cut the top of the cake flat, then turn it over. Measure the depth and circumference and brush with jam. Roll marzipan to 2 LS thick. Cut a piece to fit round the cake then roll the cake along, as shown.

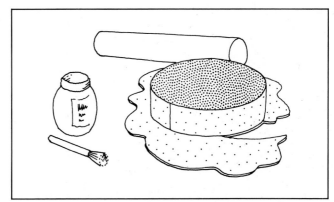

2. Brush the top with jam. Roll marzipan to 2 LS thick, lay the cake on top, then carefully cut round.
   Leave the cake to dry for 48 hours.

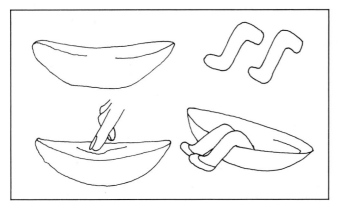

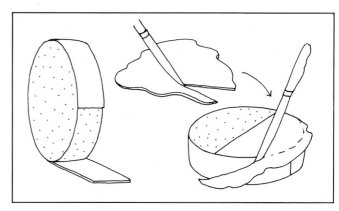

3. Take a little white fondant, add yellow and model the hammock – indent the centre with finger and pinch the edges thin to give appearance fo fabric. Model two brown legs with feet, bend them at the knee. Attach legs inside hammock with egg white. Paint black shoes. Leave to dry on a dusted surface.

4. Colour 340g (¾lb) of fondant green. Cover cake sides exactly as for marzipan, but using egg white instead of jam. Brush half the cake top with egg white. Roll green trimming (2 LS thick) to rough semi-circle shape, then cut a straight side with knife. Lay fondant on cake and trim edges.

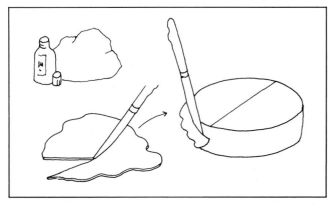

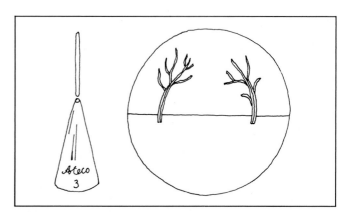

5. Take 170g (6oz) of fondant. Partially mix in blue colouring. Roll (2 LS thick) to a rough semi-circle shape and, as before, cut a straight side with knife. Lay fondant on cake and trim edges.

6. With *No. 3 nozzle* and dark brown icing, pipe bending tree trunks with several branches, as shown, about 50mm (2in.) in from each side and the trunks entending about 15mm (½in.) over the green fondant.

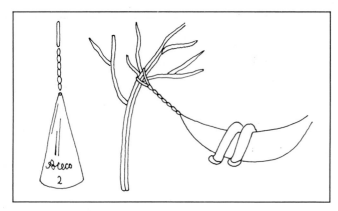

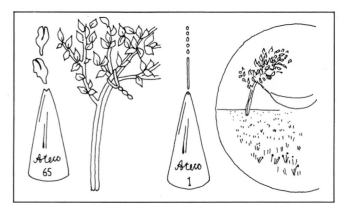

7. Position the hammock between the trees at a slight angle. Secure with icing. With *No. 2 nozzle* and yellow icing, pipe ropes from hammock to each tree trunk, as shown.

8. With *No. 65* and two shades of green in the icing bag, pipe leaves on trees. With *No. 1* and darkish green, pipe blades of grass, some clumped together, getting larger towards the forefront. Work to within 30mm (1½in.) of the cake edge. Using same nozzle and white icing, pipe little flowers (getting larger as before) on the grass.

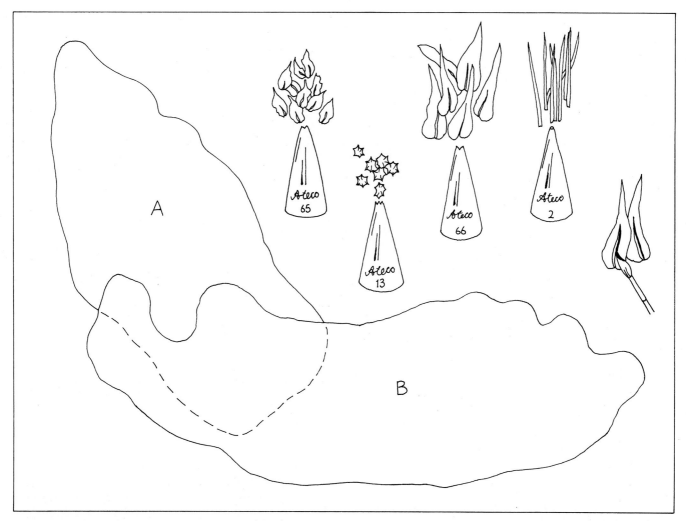

9. Roll green fondant trimmings to 1 LS thick. Cut out the shapes as shown above, Cut two **A** and **B**. Put the shapes on a dusted surface. With *No. 65* and dark green icing, cover the **A** pieces with leaves. Using *No. 13* and pink and mauve icing, pipe flowers of varying sizes between the leaves.

10. With *No. 66* and *No. 2* pipe grass and long leaves on shape **B**. (Vary the greens by adding more or less blue, yellow or red.) When the leaves are dry, paint lines of darker green at each side of the leaf vein.

Leave the pieces to dry overnight.

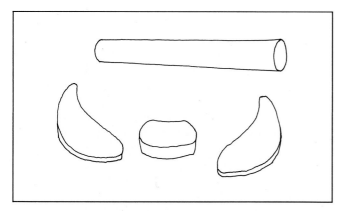

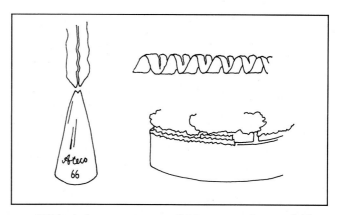

11. Mix green and blue fondant trimmings and roll to 2 LS thick. Cut out two supports for the two **A** shapes. Attach these with egg white to the cake, then attach the shapes. Roll fondant to 6 LS thick. Cut a support for shape **B** and attach as before.

12. With dark green icing and *No. 66 nozzle* pipe folding ribbons over the seams under the shapes – pipe two under **B** and one each under the two **A's**.

Mother's day

Mother's Day, celebrated on the middle Sunday of Lent, is believed to have originated from an old custom when Christians went to their Mother, or Parish, church to make special offerings. Later it became a holiday when all children who had left the family would come home to visit their mother and eat amongst other things, 'mothering cakes'. Today greetings cards and flowers are usually given as a token of appreciation and, in certain fortunate cases, Mother is presented with breakfast in bed and spends the rest of the day being pampered and spoiled by a doting husband and children.

The cake is a 200mm (8in.) square. The ingredients are given on page 127, and the method of baking, with instructions for making royal icing, fondant and marzipan, is given on page 6–7.

The cake can be decorated in a day, after the covering of marzipan has been left to dry for 48 hours.

Please read the General Notes on pages 6 or 9 before starting. Also read through the step-by-step instructions and check the ingredient and equipment lists.

Ingredients for fondant and royal icing

670g (1½lb) icing sugar, plus 60g (2oz)
1½ egg whites, plus ¼
3 tblsp liquid glucose
flavouring (optional)
Also: 560g (1¼lb) marzipan; warm sieved apricot jam; 50/50 mixture of cornflour and icing sugar in a dusting dredger; yellow, green, orange, blue, flesh, red and gold food colouring.

Equipment

Mixing bowls; spoons; sieve; rolling pin; steel rule; sharp-pointed knife; lolly sticks (LS) as spacers; pastry brush; small paint brush; greaseproof paper; Ateco (or equivalent) icing nozzle 2, 2, 3 and 44; waxed paper; heart-shaped cocktail cutter; smooth metal skewers; 250mm (10in.) square silver cake board.

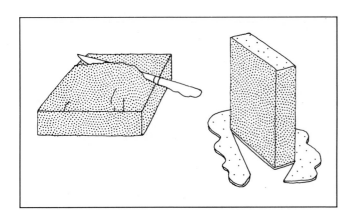

1. Cut the top of the cake flat, then turn it over. Roll marzipan to 2 LS thick. Brush two opposite sides of cake with jam. Lay one side on marzipan and cut round. Repeat with other side, and then with the two remaining sides.

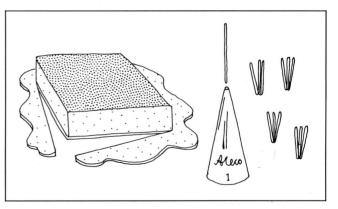

2. Brush top of the cake with jam. Roll marzipan to 2 LS thick. Lay cake on and cut round. Leave to dry for 48 hours.

Meanwhile make the royal icing. With *No. 1 nozzle* pipe the stamen (in threes, as shown) on waxed paper.

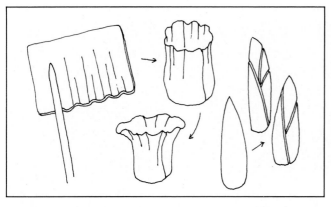

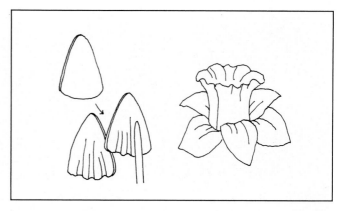

3. Colour 45g (1½oz) of fondant yellow. Flatten a small piece to roughly 20mm x 30mm (¾in. x 1¼in.). Mark it with the skewer. Bend it round to form a tube, nip seams together and curl the top out with fingers. Make eight. Paint frilled edges of three with orange. Model four buds, marking down sides with sharp knife.

4. Add a little white fondant to yellow – to make paler petals. Model six petals for each of four flowers and five each for remainder (these will be positioned sideways). Attach to tube with egg white, three first, then three underneath. Leave to dry.

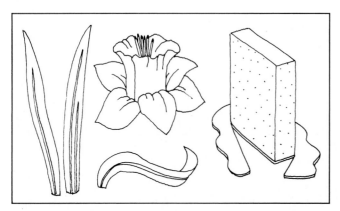

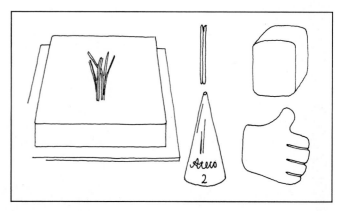

5. Roll 15g (½oz) of green fondant very thin. Cut seven leaves and mark with knife. Curl some, then leave to dry. Pipe a blob of icing into trumpet of each flower and position stamen. Paint tips yellow. Cover the cake with fondant, exactly as with marzipan, but using egg white instead of jam.

6. Position cake on board. With green icing and *No. 2 nozzle* pipe double lined stalks. Leave for 30 minutes. Model parcel from 30g (1oz) of blue fondant. Model hands (marking fingers with blunt edge of knife), from just under 60g (2oz) of flesh fondant. Attach leaves, buds and flowers, using green icing to secure.

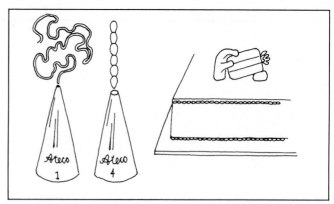

7. With *No. 44* pipe ribbon and bow on parcel. Roll a little red fondant to 1 LS thick. Cut out heart. With *No. 1* pipe *Mother, Mummy* or *Mama* etc. Pipe continuous dots round edge. Measure 50mm (2in.) out from cake corner and using a cup, mark a quarter circle. Pipe this with *No. 1*, then three more outside it.

8. Fill the centre circle with squiggly lines. Paint ribbon and edge of heart gold. With *No. 4* pipe continuous dots round base and top of cake. Tilt parcel forwards (support with white fondant) and secure with icing. Position hands, and the heart, securing with neat blobs of icing.

Valentine

St Valentine, a Roman priest (who was epileptic) was executed around AD 270 for his Christian faith. After his death, sufferers of epilepsy offered their prayers believing he would intercede on their behalf; but his association with love is not directly attributable to him, rather to the fact that he was killed on the eve of Lupercalia, the feast of Pan. During the Roman occupation of Britian this feast became the Spring festival but, as with other pagan customs, it was discouraged by Christians and replaced by a Saint's Day commemorating Valentine. Thus the combination of Spring, mating, new life, love and Valentine was established.

The cakes are baked in two 150mm (6in.) heart-shaped tins – use the recipe for a 150mm (6in.) round cake for each of these. Ingredients and quantities are given on page 127 and the method for baking on page 6–7. Instructions for making royal icing, marzipan and fondant are on page 7.

The cake will take two days to decorate, after the covering of marzipan has been left to dry for 48 hours. (If the filling-in and filigree, captions 5 to 10, are made during the 48 hours, the cake can be completed in three days.)

Please read the General Notes on pages 6 to 9 before starting to decorate. Also read through the step-by-step instructions and check the ingredient and equipment lists.

Ingredients for fondant and royal icing

670g (1½lb) icing sugar, plus 220g (½lb)
1½ egg whites, plus ½
3 tblsp liquid glucose
flavouring (optional)
Also: 670g (1½lb) marzipan; warm sieved apricot jam; 50/50 mixture of cornflour and icing sugar in a dusting dredger; red and gold food colouring.

Equipment

Mixing bowls; spoons; sieve; rolling pin; steel rule; sharp-pointed knife; lolly sticks (LS) as spacers; pastry brush; small paint brush; greaseproof paper; Ateco (or equivalent) icing nozzles 1, 2, 3, 4 and 61; stiff card; tracing paper; adhesive tape; waxed paper; skewer; two 200mm (8in.) silver heart-shaped cake boards.

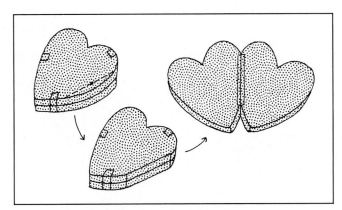

1. Tape the two boards, backs together, as shown. Mark 10mm (⅜in.) at the point shown, then draw a straight 115mm (4½in.) line. Cut along the line with a serrated bread knife or saw. Remove tape. Tape boards together securely underneath, then turn over and stick a narrow piece of tin foil over the join with clear tape on the top.

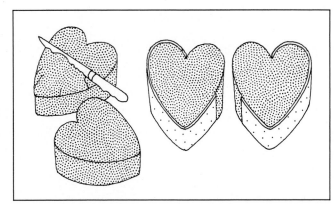

2. Slice the tops of the cakes flat, then turn over. Roll marzipan to 2 LS thick. Brush sides of one cake with jam. Cut marzipan to same depth as cake and 380mm (15in.) long, then apply. Cut and apply a piece to fit remaining area. Repeat with other cake, placing join at facing side, as shown.

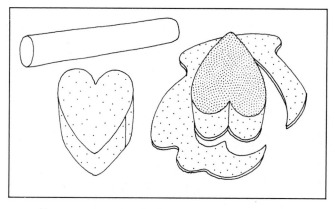

3. Roll marzipan to 2 LS thick. Brush cake tops with jam. Lay cakes on and cut neatly to shape.
    Leave both to dry for 48 hours.

4. Take 450g (1lb) of fondant. Cover sides of cakes exactly as with marzipan, but using egg white instead of jam. Add 220g ($\frac{1}{2}$lb) of fondant to trimmings and knead in red colouring. Roll to 2 LS thick. Brush a thin film of egg white on top of cakes, lay fondant on and neatly trim edges.

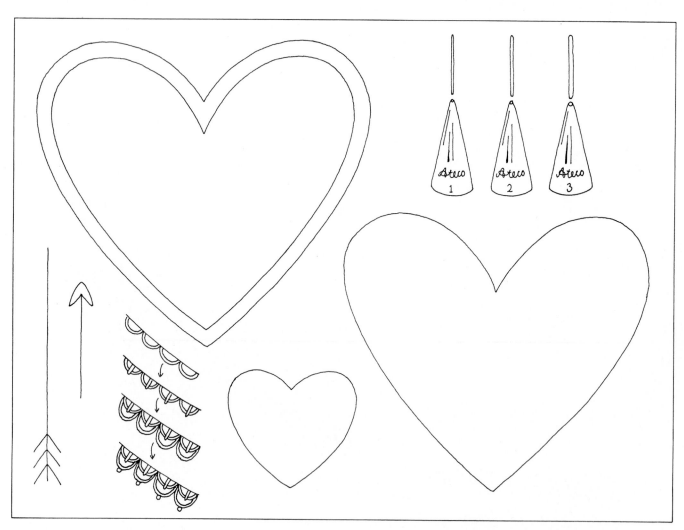

5. Make the royal icing.
    Trace the large heart on to two pieces of card, the small heart on to four pieces of card and the arrow pieces on to another card. Tape waxed paper over the drawings. Trace the medium heart on to card and carefully cut out (this will be used as a template).

6. Using *No. 3 nozzle* pipe the arrow shafts and small hearts. With *No. 2* pipe the two lines of the large hearts, and the arrow quills and points.
    Using *No. 1 nozzle* pipe the lace around the large hearts — pipe the small loops first, then the cross lines, the larger loops and finally the dots.

ABCDEF
GHIJKLM
NOPQRST
UVWXYZ

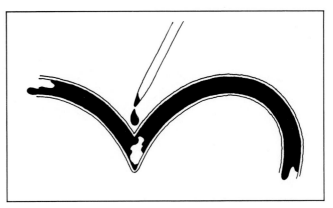

7. Trace two appropriate initials on to stiff card, tape waxed paper over as before. Pipe the outlines with *No. 1* then leave to dry for an hour.

8. Using the same nozzle, fill in the letters to give a baroque effect by following the curved lines and piping zigzag lines on parallel parts, as shown.

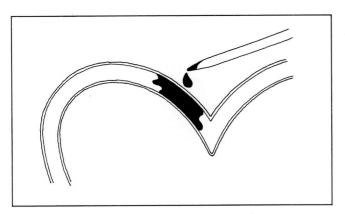

9. Add a little water to three tablespoons of icing. Using a skewer, carefully fill in the double lines of the large hearts. Use a teaspoon and skewer to fill in the small hearts. Leave to dry for 24 hours.

10. If small holes appear (particularly at the centre points of the large hearts, for some reason) wait until the icing has completely dried, then carefully fill in with a little blob of the watered icing on the end of the skewer.

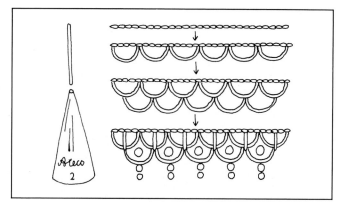

11. Roll the red fondant trimmings to 1 LS thick. Place the template on top and neatly cut out two hearts. Leave to dry on a dusted surface.

Model five supports for the hearts, as shown – the large ones 20mm (¾in.) high and the small ones 15mm (½in.) high.

12. Using *nozzle No. 2* pipe white lace around the two cakes. Start with a line of continuous dots along the fondant seams, then pipe the loops, cross lines, and finally the dots.

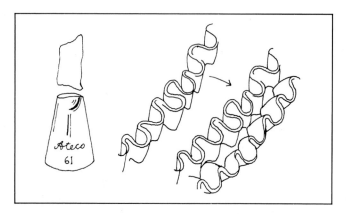

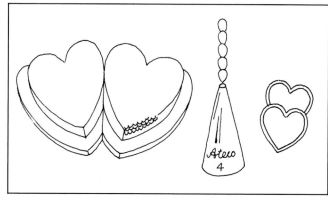

13. Keep a little white icing, and colour the remainder pale pink. With *nozzle No. 61* pipe a frill (with nozzle narrow end upwards) around top edge of both cakes. Add a little more red to icing and pipe another frill from the base of the previous one. Leave to dry for an hour.

14. Position the cakes on the boards, securing them with a smear of icing. Add more red to the icing and pipe a frill, attaching slightly under the previous one. Using *No. 4*, pipe continuous dots around base of cakes.

Stick two hearts together with a blob of icing. Leave to dry for 30 minutes.

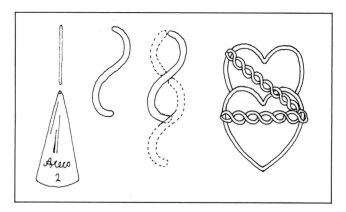

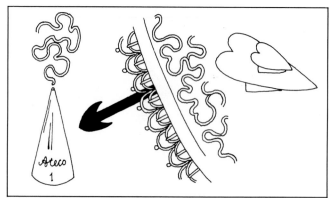

15. With *No. 2 nozzle* pipe a chain, as shown, across the hearts. Paint arrows, letters, chain and hearts' outlines gold. Attach letters with dabs of icing. Very carefully peel waxed paper from large hearts. Pipe around edge of red hearts and – very, very carefully – position the lace hearts.

16. With *No. 1*, pipe squiggly lines on the hearts.

Position arrows (pointed end underneath, as shown) on heart swith neat dabs of icing. Secure the little supports and attach the small hearts with icing. Secure the large supports and carefully attach the large hearts.

Midsummer

There are many themes which would happily cover this subject – characters from Shakespeare's *A Midsummer Night's Dream*; or some crazy scene depicting Midsummer madness, Druids and Stonehenge; but as midnight barbecues are a good way of celebrating I thought a charcoal grill would make an interesting design for a cake. Having sweet replicas of the real thing may cause slight confusion, particularly at the party's end when the alcohol has been flowing freely but, so much the better. You might even flavour the culinary fakes – banana kebabs, almond sausages, strawberry drumsticks.

The grill is made from a 230mm (9in.) square cake. Ingredients and quantities for this are given on page 127 and the method for baking on page 6–7. Instructions for making royal icing, marzipan and fondant are given on page 7. If you are making your own fondant, you may find it easier to make the 1.120kg (2½lb) in two batches, keeping each piece securely wrapped in cling film and in an airtight container until required.

The cake can be decorated in a day, after the covering of marzipan has been left to dry for 48 hours. It always helps when copying food in fondant, to have some form of reference, either a good colour photograph from a magazine or cookery book, or the real thing.

Please read the General Notes on pages 6 to 9 before starting to decorate. Also read through the step-by-step instructions and check the ingredient and equipment lists.

Ingredients for fondant and royal icing

1.120kg (2½lb) icing sugar, plus 110g (4oz)
2½ egg whites, plus ½
5 tblsp liquid glucose
flavouring (optional)
Also: 560g (1¼lb) marzipan; warm sieved apricot jam; 50/50 mixture of cornflour and icing sugar in a dusting dredger; black, red, orange, yellow, blue, green and silver food colouring.

Equipment

Mixing bowls; spoons; sieve; rolling pin; steel rule; sharp-pointed knife; lolly sticks (LS) as spacers; pastry brush; small paint brush; greaseproof paper; Ateco (or equivalent) icing nozzles 3 and 4; stiff white card; waxed paper; adhesive tape; 300mm (12in.) square silver cake board.

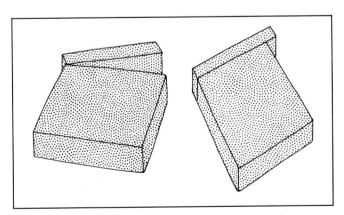

1. Slice the top of the cake flat, then turn over. Cut a 25mm (1in.) piece from one side and attach to the other, as shown, with jam and a sliver of marzipan. Trim off the excess.

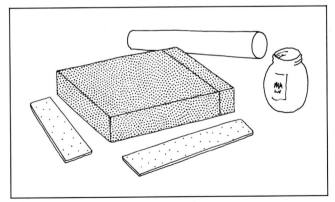

2. Roll marzipan to 2 LS thick. Measure the sides of the cake, brush with jam, cut marzipan to fit, then apply. Measure top, brush with jam, cut marzipan to fit, then apply. Leave to dry for 48 hours.

3. Take 450g (1lb) of fondant. Break off two lumps. Partially mix red and orange into one. Add black to the other to make dark grey, then partially mix in more black to give streaky effect. Colour the remaining fondant grey.

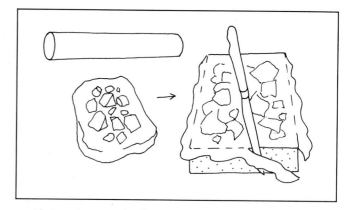

4. Flatten the grey fondant to an oblong half the size of the cake. Dot with pieces of red and dark grey, as shown, then roll everything to 2 LS thick. Brush the cake top with a thin film of egg white, apply fondant and neatly trim the edges.

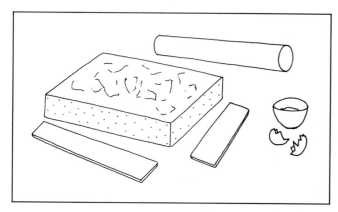

5. Mix 220g (8oz) of fondant in with the trimmings and add a little red. Cover cake sides exactly as for marzipan, but using egg white instead of jam.
    Make the royal icing.

6. Using a ruler and sharp knife, mark the grid on the charcoal surface. Mark the lines at 13mm ($\frac{1}{2}$in.) intervals. With *No. 4 nozzle* and black icing, pipe along the scored lines.

7. Roll fondant trimmings to 2 LS thick. Cut strips 10mm ($\frac{3}{8}$in.) wide to fit around edge of cake. Secure them in position with egg white. Roll pieces of white fondant, 1 LS thick, to fit each corner – pieces should be about 20mm ($\frac{7}{8}$in.) wide. Attach with egg white and trim inside corners.

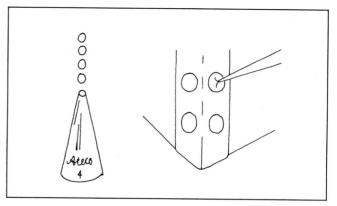

8. With *No. 4 nozzle* and white icing, pipe screw heads on the corner pieces. (As each head is piped, gently push the point of the icing back into the blob with the end of a wet knife – this gives a perfectly round and smooth surface.)

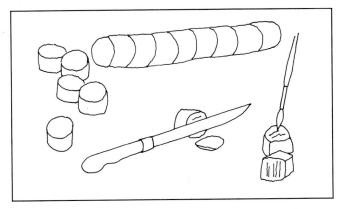

9. Take about 150g (5oz) of fondant, add yellow, brown and blue, a little at a time until meat colour is reached. Form a roll and cut into 13 rough pieces. Make the texture by using a sawing motion with knife when cutting off the smooth surface. Paint brown on the meat to accentuate grain.

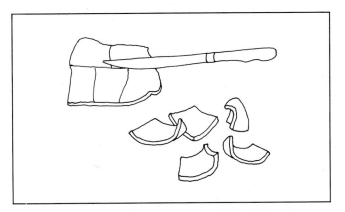

10. Add red to trimmings. Flatten and cut into five pieces, as shown. Bend slightly. Add green to some white fondant and make four pieces of green pepper, as with red.

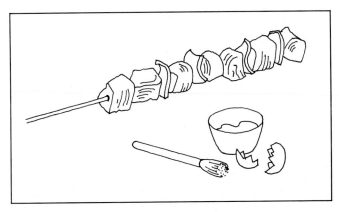

11. Push meat and peppers together, securing with egg white. Pierce both ends of each row with a skewer. Leave on a dusted surface overnight.

12. Draw the skewer pieces on to stiff card, then tape waxed paper over the drawings. With *nozzle No. 3* and white icing pipe the lines 40mm (1½in.) long, trailing to make a point at the end. Pipe the lines with loops on the end, as shown. Leave to dry overnight.

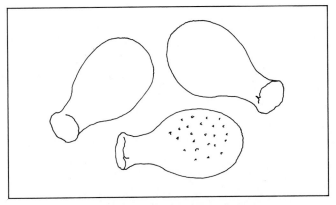

13. Take about 150g (5oz) of fondant. Colour with a little yellow and brown to make a creamy fawn. Divide into three, and model the drumsticks, as shown. Make the textured skin by rolling a nutmeg grater over the surfaces.

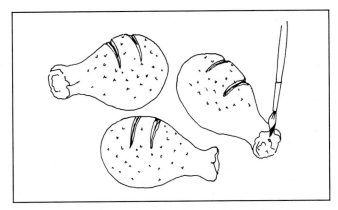

14. Make the grill marks with the paint brush handle. Paint the joint area roughly with brown. Mix yellow with a little brown and paint areas of the drumsticks. Paint brown in the grill marks, and uneven spots of brown all over the surface. Leave to dry.

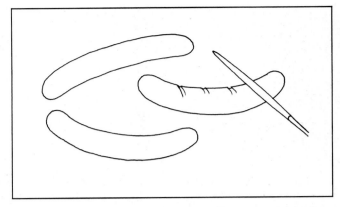

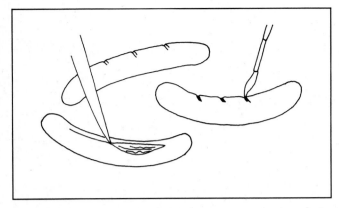

15. Add a little brown and red to the remaining white fondant. Divide into three and roll smooth sausages. Bend them slightly. Make grill marks with paint brush handle.

16. Mix red and a little brown and brush areas of the sausages. Paint grill marks with brown. Leave to dry for 30 minutes, then split one of the sausages and pull apart carefully. Leave to dry overnight.

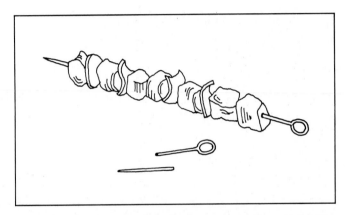

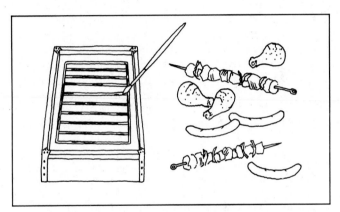

17. Paint the corners of the barbecue pan silver. Paint the skewer pieces while they are still on the waxed paper. When dry, carefully peel off the waxed paper. Pipe icing into the holes in the pieces of meat, then carefully push in the skewers.

18. Paint the grill (partially, to give the appearance of being charred) with silver.
    Position the food. Leave loose, or secure with neat blobs of icing.

Christmas

It is generally believed that the first Christmas tree was erected in the eighth century by St Boniface, a Christian missionary in Germany. He set up a fir tree to replace the oak which was sacred to the pagan god Thor, and then decorated it with offerings to the child Jesus. The German reformer, Martin Luther, is thought to have started the custom of lighting the tree with candles. Queen Victoria's husband, Albert of Saxe-Coburg, introduced the tree to England and German immigrants took the idea to America.

The tree is made from four 130mm (5in.), one 150mm (6in.) and one 180mm (7in.) round cakes. Ingredients for these are given on page 127 and method for baking on page 6–7. Instructions for making royal icing, marzipan and fondant are given on page 7. If you make your own fondant, it will be easier to make the 1.230kg (2¾lb) in three batches, keeping it securely wrapped in cling film and in an airtight container.

The tree can be completed in a day, but the covering of marzipan must be allowed to dry for 48 hours. During this time the decorations can be made.

The candle holders must be pliable plastic, so that they can be cut and bent without snapping. If these are unavailable rigid plastic ones can be used, but they will have to be stuck into the tree at an angle.

Please read the General Notes on pages 6 to 9 before starting to decorate. Also read through the step-by-step instructions and check the ingredient and equipment lists.

Ingredients for fondant and royal icing

1.230kg (2¾lb) icing sugar, plus 280g (10oz)
2¾ egg whites, plus 1¼
5½ tblsp liquid glucose
flavouring (optional)
Also: 1kg (2¼lb) marzipan; warm sieved apricot jam; 50/50 mixture of cornflour and icing sugar in a dusting dredger; green, red and gold food colouring; edible lustre powder.

Equipment

Mixing bowls; spooons; sieve; rolling pin; steel rule; sharp-pointed knife; lolly sticks (LS) as spacers; pastry brush; small paint brush; greaseproof paper; Ateco (or equivalent) icing nozzles 1, 2 and 3; 15 pliable plastic candles; oil-based gold paint (for candle holders); 15 red candles; 230mm (9in.) round silver cake board; tracing paper; stiff white card; waxed paper; adhesive tape.

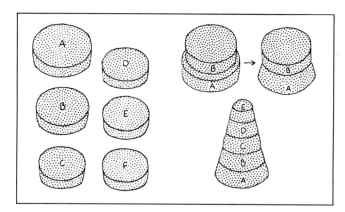

1. Slice the tops of the cakes flat. Brush top of **A** and underside of **B** with jam. Lay a sliver of marzipan on **A** and put **B** on top. Trim sides of **A** sloping in to the bottom of **B**, as shown. Brush top of **B** and underside of **C**, repeat as with **A** and **B**. Trim **D** and **E** to make the conical shape shown.

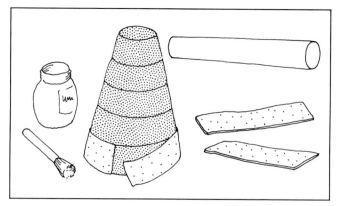

2. Apply marzipan in strips as shown – measure circumference of bottom of cake, roll marzipan to 2 LS thick. Brush area of cake with jam and apply strips. Continue until sides are covered. Roll marzipan to 1 LS thick. Brush bottom of tree with jam, then stand cake on marzipan and cut round.

114

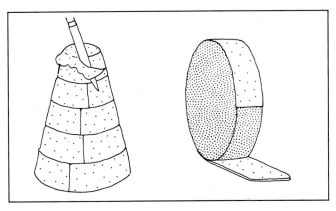

3. Brush top with jam, lay on a piece of marzipan 1 LS thick, and trim edges. Measure sides of **F**, brush with jam. Roll marzipan to 2 LS thick, cut to size, then roll cake along.

Leave both cakes to dry (the tree on a generously dusted surface) for 48 hours.

4. Meanwhile, make the decorations. Trace the snowflakes below on to tracing paper, then on to pieces of stiff card. Tape pieces of waxed paper over the drawings. Using *No. 2 nozzle* first, for the solid lines, and *No. 1* for the broken lines, pipe three snowflakes.

5. Carefully remove tape and slide waxed paper on to another flat surface. Put some fresh waxed paper on to the card and repeat piping. Make fifteen snowflakes in all. Trace fairy's wings on to tracing paper, then on to stiff card. Cover with waxed paper as before and, using *nozzles 2* and *1* (*No. 1* for broken lines), pipe the wings. (Pipe two sets of wings, then choose the better.) Repeat tracing and piping method, using *No. 2* for wand (pipe two) and stars (pipe twenty). Leave all to dry for 24 hours, then paint half the stars, wand and edges of wings with gold. Use paint brush to dust remaining stars with lustre powder.

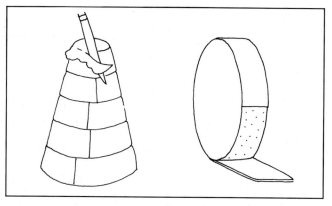

6. Colour 900g (2lb) of fondant green. Apply to tree exactly as for marzipan, but using egg white instead of jam. Colour 200g (7oz) of fondant red and cover base, as for marzipan. When applied, mark vertical lines with blunt edge of knife.

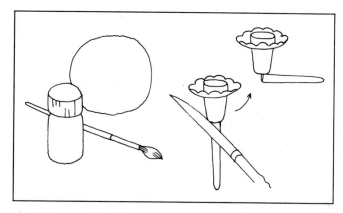

7. Make round baubles with remaining red fondant and dust with lustre powder.

Cut a knick at the top of each candle holder stem. Bend stem backwards, then paint with oil-based gold.

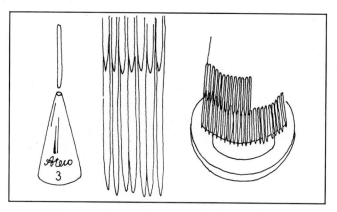

8. Attach base to tree with egg white, then base to the cake board with a blob of icing.

With *No. 3 nozzle* pipe pine needles on tree. Work five rows, starting at bottom and working up. Take the nozzle down, dragging to make a point at the bottom as shown.

9. Model a support from green fondant trimmings, about 60mm ($2\frac{1}{4}$in.) high. Attach to centre top of tree with icing. Roll white fondant to 1 LS thick and cut a 130mm (5in.) circle, lay it over support, attaching with egg white. Cut another circle, about 60mm ($2\frac{1}{2}$in.) and attach over large one.

10. Model body, neck and head, as shown, then attach. Push wand into waist, then model arms and attach. With *No. 2 nozzle* pipe loops around edges of dress and neck, then pipe eyes and hair. Pipe a line of icing down the back and attach wings.

Dust fairy with lustre powder and paint piping gold. Melt bottom of candles and push into holders. Carefully push holders into sides of tree, secure the lip of each holder at back with a neat blob of green icing.

Carefully peel waxed paper from back of snowflakes and stars. Pipe a blob of green icing where a snowflake is to be positioned, then very carefully lift snowflake and secure to tree. Repeat for remaining snowflakes and stars. Attach baubles in the same way, holding each one for a little while until it feels secure.

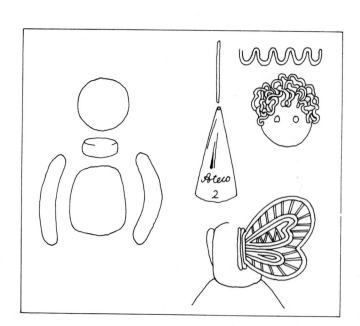

Easter

Easter, the Christian festival commemorating the resurrection of Christ, was originally an eight-day festival held in April for Easter, the Saxon goddess of the east. April was called Ostermonath – the month of the east wind – and Easter Sunday, regulated by the paschal moon, must be celebrated between 21 March and 25 April. Easter eggs are symbols of creation, or the re-creation of spring. The practice of giving eggs (real ones, not chocolate) came from Persia (Iran); the custom was also part of Jewish, Egyptian and Hindu tradition. Christians adopted the custom in order to symbolise the resurrection.

The window is made from a 260mm (10in.) square cake. Ingredients and quantities for this are given on page 127 and the method of baking on page 6–7. Instructions for making royal icing, marzipan and fondant are also on page 7. If you are making your own fondant, you may find it easier to make the 1.120kg (2½lb) in two batches, keeping each piece securely wrapped in cling film and in an airtight container until required.

The cake can be decorated in two days, after the covering of marzipan has been left to dry for 48 hours. The window scene is very easy – areas of piped icing are filled in with watered icing and left to dry.

Please read the General Notes on pages 6 to 9 before starting to decorate. Also read through the step-by-step instructions and check the ingredient and equipment lists.

Ingredients for fondant and royal icing

1.120kg (2½lb) icing sugar, plus 220g (8oz)
2½ egg whites, plus 1
5 tblsp liquid glucose
flavouring (optional)
Also: 800g (1¾lb) marzipan; warm sieved apricot jam; 50/50 mixture of cornflour and icing sugar in a dusting dredger; green, brown, yellow, blue, red, and gold food colouring.

Equipment

Mixing bowls; spoons; sieve; rolling pin; steel rule; sharp-pointed knife; lolly sticks (LS) as spacers; pastry brush; small paint brush; greaseproof paper; Ateco (or equivalent) icing nozzles 1, 2, 4 and 78; graph paper; tracing paper; sewing needle; waxed paper; metal skewer.

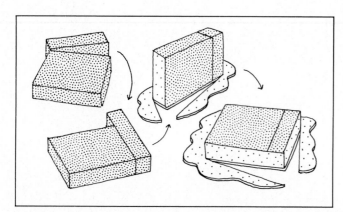

1. Slice the top of the cake flat. Cut off a 50mm (2in.) slab and attach to narrow end, using jam and a sliver of marzipan to secure. Trim the edge piece. Roll marzipan to 2 LS thick. Brush cake sides with jam, then lay on the marzipan and cut round. Repeat for top, then leave to dry for 48 hours.

2. Cover cake with white fondant, exactly as for marzipan, but using a thin film of egg white instead of jam. Leave to dry overnight. Meanwhile prepare the coloured icing and store it in airtight jars – white, yellow, blue, light and dark brown, four greens – about two teaspoonsful of each.

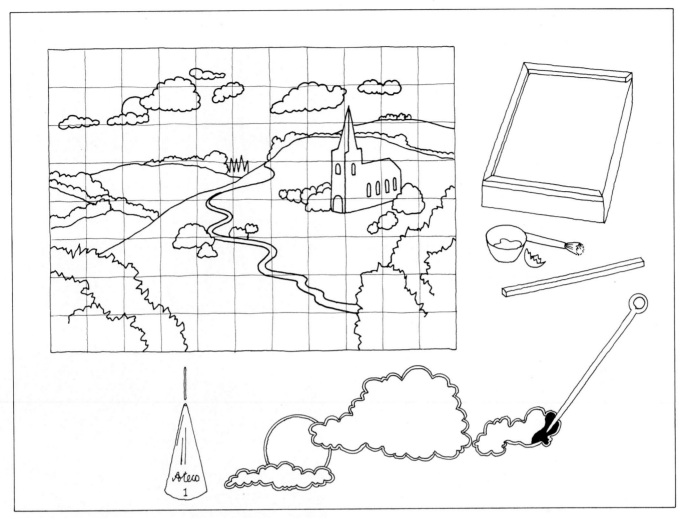

3. Copy the above drawing – each square represents 25mm (1in.) on graph paper 200mm x 300mm (8in. x 12in.) – then trace on to tracing paper. Attach part to cake top with dabs of icing, then prick through the pencil lines on to the fondant. Remove tracing. Roll fondant trimmings to 3 LS thick and cut strips 10mm ($\frac{3}{8}$in.) wide to fit the four sides.

Using *nozzle No. 1* pipe the outlines in this sequence, white clouds, yellow sun, light brown front of church with dark brown side, bushes and fields in various greens. Water the colours (not too runny) and use a small spoon or skewer to guide the icing into inaccessible areas.

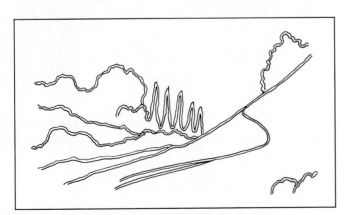

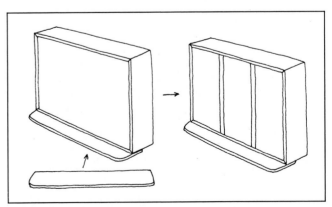

4. Fill in the sky first, pale blue running into white. Fill fields with dark brown and shades of green. Fill hedges, greens running into browns, then fill foreground foliage. Fill sun, clouds, and finally, using tiny blobs of colour, fill in the stained-glass church windows. Leave to dry for two hours.

5. Roll fondant trimmings to 3 LS thick. Cut window ledge 25mm (1in.) wide. Round off two facing corners and attach with egg white to bottom of cake. Roll fondant to 2 LS thick. Cut two strips for inside of frame, just under 10mm ($\frac{3}{8}$in.) wide. Position 100mm (4in.) from outer edges.

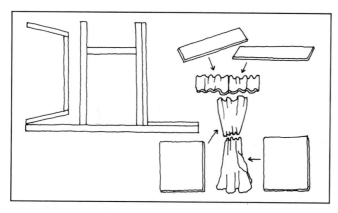

6. Roll fondant to 1 LS thick. Cut pieces for windows, as shown and position with egg white. Colour 220g (8oz) of fondant pink. Roll to 1 LS thick. Cut, gather and position two pieces 90mm ($3\frac{1}{2}$in.) square and two 90mm x 120mm ($3\frac{1}{2}$in. x $4\frac{3}{4}$in.) as shown. Cut, gather and attach the frill 25mm (1in.) deep, in pieces, as shown.

7. Add blue to trimmings and model the vase. Add green to trimmings and model stem support. Attach support to vase. With *No. 2* pipe the stems, with *No. 78* pipe flowers. Add brown to trimmings and model Easter egg. Flatten two pieces of white fondant. Position one on the sill and one around the egg.

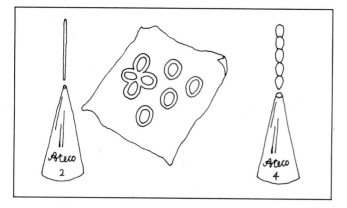

8. Paint the wrapping gold. With *No. 2* pipe the string. Pipe the bow parts on waxed paper. When dry, carefully peel off and secure with a blob of icing in the centre of the main bow. Paint gold when dry and attach to string. With *No. 4* pipe a row of continuous dots around base of cake.

Cornucopia – Harvest Festival/Thanksgiving

The Cornucopia, or Horn of Plenty, was originally part of Greek mythology – Amalthea, one of the daughters of the Cretan king, once fed the infant Zeus with goat's milk. In gratitude Zeus gave her the goat's horn and promised that whoever possessed it would have everything in abundance he or she desired. We have adopted the symbol and use it to represent the rich collection of produce gathered at harvest time.

The base and horn are made from a 200mm (8in.) square cake and a 180mm (7in.) round cake. Ingredients and quantities for these are given on page 127 and the method of baking of page 6–7. Instructions for making royal icing, marzipan and fondant are on page 7. If you are making your own fondant, you may find it easier to make the 1.120kg ($2\frac{1}{2}$lb) in two batches, keeping each piece securely wrapped in cling film and in an airtight container until required.

The cake will take one to two days to decorate, after the covering of marzipan has been left to dry for 48 hours. It always helps when copying food in fondant, to have some form of reference, either a good colour photograph from a magazine or cookery book, or the real thing.

Please read the General Notes on pages 6 to 9 before starting to decorate. Also read through the step-to-step instructions and check the ingredient and equipment lists.

Ingredients for fondant and royal icing

1.120kg ($2\frac{1}{2}$lb) icing sugar, plus 110g (4oz)
$2\frac{1}{2}$ egg whites, plus $\frac{1}{2}$
5 tblsp liquid glucose
flavouring (optional)
Also: 800g ($1\frac{3}{4}$lb) marzipan; warm sieved apricot jam; 50/50 mixture of cornflour and icing sugar in a dusting dredger; yellow, black, red, green, brown and blue food colouring.

Equipment

Mixing bowls; spoons; sieve; rolling pin; steel rule; sharp-pointed knife; lolly sticks (LS) to use as spacers; pastry brush; small paint brush; greaseproof paper; Ateco (or equivalent) icing nozzles 2 and 4; stiff card; adhesive tape; waxed paper; smooth metal skewer or knitting needle; nutmeg grater; 280mm (11in.) square silver cake board.

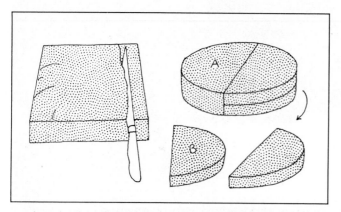

1. Slice the top of the cakes flat. Turn the square one over and cut the round one in half. Slice one of the halves in half, as shown (only one of these will be required).

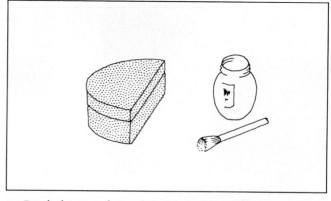

2. Brush the top of **A** and the underside of **B** with jam. Stick them together with a sliver of marzipan in between.

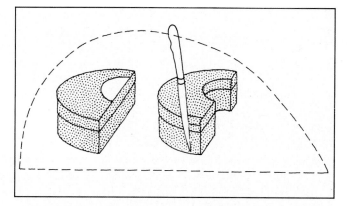

3. Trace the above shape on to card and use it as a guide. Position it 75mm (3in.) along from the corner of the semi-circle cake, as shown, and cut carefully around. Trim a little bit of cake from the square corners of the top and underside, so that the edges are rounded.

4. Measure the sides of the square cake. Brush with jam then roll marzipan to 2 LS thick. Cut to size, then apply. Roll marzipan to 2 LS thick, brush cake top with jam, lay it on the marzipan and cut round, as shown.

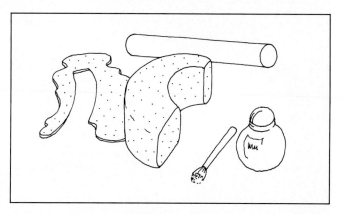

5. Roll marzipan to 2 LS thick. Brush top of horn with jam and cut marzipan to fit. Measure the front and back of horn, brush with jam and apply marzipan, smoothing over the joins with hands. Cover the ends as with top of square cake.
   Leave both cakes to dry for 48 hours.

6. Meanwhile, make the fruits. The 6 apples, 6 tomatoes and 2 bunches of grapes are made from just under 220g (8oz) of fondant. Use about 22g ($\frac{3}{4}$oz) for each apple, colour two of them pale green, four a darker green. Roll to a smooth ball, indent centre with thumb, then pierce with skewer, as shown.

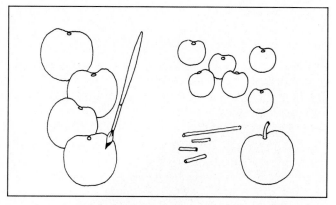

7. When the dark apples are dry, paint areas of streaky red. Colour 30g (1oz) of fondant red, roll the tomatoes, then indent and pierce the centres. Colour 30g (1oz) of fondant dark brown. Roll a thin piece and cut into stalks. Leave until dry, then brush ends with egg white and push into apples.

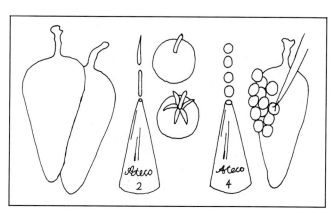

8. Model the remaining brown into 2 grape-bunches, with stalks, as shown. With *No. 2 nozzle*, pipe green stalks in tomato holes, then leaves. Lay grape bunches on waxed paper. With *No. 4* pipe and purple (red and blue mixed) icing, pipe the grapes. As each grape is piped, push point of icing back into blob with a wet knife.

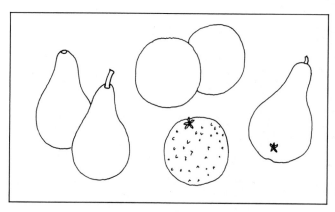

9. Model 3 pears yellowy-green, and pierce tops as before. Roll stalks and attach when dry. With just over 60g (2oz) of fondant model 3 oranges. Roll each one over nutmeg grater. With *No. 2* pipe brown calyx on each orange and on underside of one pear.

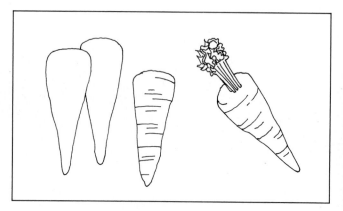

10. Colour 30g (1oz) of fondant bright orange and model seven carrots. Mark horizontal lines across each with a sharp knife. Lay them on waxed paper and, with *No. 2* and green icing, pipe stalks 20mm ($\frac{3}{4}$in.) long, ending with rough foliage. Push nozzle down, then up, to form little peaks.

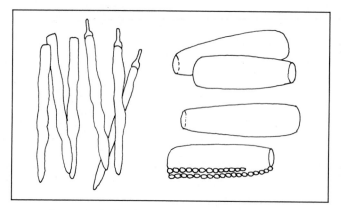

11. Colour a little fondant green and make bumpy rolls for beans, pointed at one end, flat at the top. With *No. 2* pipe stems. Colour 15g ($\frac{1}{2}$oz) of fondant yellow. Roll 4 corn cob shapes. Place on waxed paper and, with *No. 2* and fairly stiff yellow icing, pipe lines of corn.

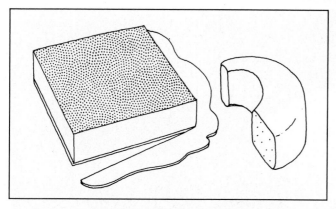

12. Colour 670g (1½lb) of fondant pale yellow. Cover the square cake exactly as for marzipan – caption 4, but using egg white instead of jam. Add 220g (½lb) to trimmings, then partially mix in a little black to give a streaky appearance. Cover the top, front, back and narrow end of horn exactly as for marzipan.

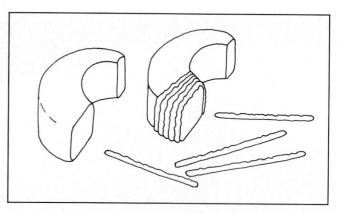

13. Add more black to a piece of fondant and cover large end of horn. Form the remaining fondant into rolls, attach to horn with egg white. Mark grooves with a knife handle.

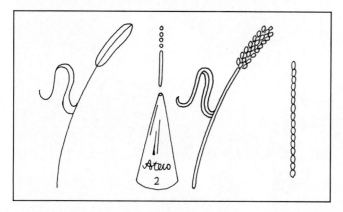

14. Trace the drawing above on to greaseproof paper. Prick through pencil lines with a sewing needle on to the cake sides – 5 on each side at 20mm (¾in.) intervals. With *No. 2* and pale yellow icing, pipe the corn. Pipe continuous dots along top and bottom edges and down each corner of cake.

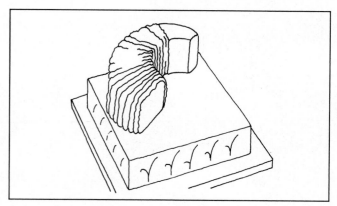

15. Position the horn on the cake, securing it with neat blobs of icing. Carefully position the fruit and vegetables, again securing with dabs of icing.

Rich fruit cake

	130mm(5in) square cake and 150mm(6in) round cake	150mm(6in) square cake and 180mm(7in) round cake	180mm(7in) square cake and 200mm(8in) round cake	200mm(8in) square cake and 230mm(9in) round cake	230mm(9in) square cake and 250mm(10in) round cake	250mm(10in) square cake and 280mm(11in) round cake	280mm(11in) square cake and 300mm(12in) round cake	300mm(12in) square cake and 330mm(13in) round cake
Currants	110g(4oz)	170g(6oz)	280g(10oz)	360g(13oz)	500g(18oz)	670g(24oz)	900g(32oz)	1.4kg(48oz)
Raisins	80g(3oz)	140g(5oz)	200g(7oz)	280g(10oz)	360g(10oz)	530g(19oz)	620g(22oz)	500g(18oz)
Sultanas	60g(2oz)	80g(3oz)	110g(4oz)	200g(7oz)	200g(7oz)	360g(13oz)	390g(14oz)	500g(18oz)
Chopped mixed peel	30g(1oz)	60g(20z)	60g)2oz)	80g(3oz)	110g(4oz	140g(5oz)	200g(7oz)	250g(9oz)
Glacé cherries	40g($1\frac{1}{2}$oz)	70g($2\frac{1}{2}$oz)	80g(3oz)	110g(4oz)	140g(5oz)	220g(8oz)	280g(10oz)	350g(12oz)
Chopped blanched almonds	30g(1oz)	60g(2oz)	60g(2oz)	80g(3oz)	110g(4oz)	140g(5oz)	200g(7oz)	250g(9oz)
Grated rind	$\frac{1}{2}$ lemon	$\frac{1}{2}$ lemon	$\frac{3}{4}$ lemon	1 lemon	1 lemon	1 lemon	$1\frac{1}{2}$ lemons	2 lemons
Plain flour	100g($3\frac{1}{2}$oz)	170g(6oz)	210g($7\frac{1}{2}$oz)	340g(12oz)	390g(14oz)	590g(21oz)	670g(24oz)	825g(29oz)
Ground cinnamon	$\frac{1}{2}$ teasp	$\frac{1}{2}$	$\frac{3}{4}$ teasp	1 teasp	$1\frac{1}{2}$ teas	2 teasp	$2\frac{1}{2}$ teasp	$2\frac{3}{4}$ teasp
Ground mixed spice	$\frac{1}{4}$ teasp	$\frac{1}{4}$ teasp	$\frac{1}{2}$ teasp	$\frac{3}{4}$ teasp	1 teasp	$1\frac{1}{4}$ teasp	$1\frac{1}{2}$ teasp	$1\frac{3}{4}$ teasp
Butter	80g(3oz)	140g(5oz)	170g(6oz)	280g(10oz)	340g(12oz)	500g(18oz)	590g(21oz)	800g(28oz)
Soft brown sugar	80g(3oz)	140g(5oz)	170g(6oz)	280g(10oz)	340g(12oz)	500g(18oz)	590g(21oz)	800g(28oz)
Medium eggs	$1\frac{1}{2}$	$2\frac{1}{2}$	3	5	6	9	11	14
Black treacle	1 teasp	1 teasp	1 tblsp	1 tblsp	1 tblsp	2 tblsp	2 tblsp	2 tblsp
Approx. cooking time	2 hours	$2\frac{1}{2}$ hours	$2\frac{3}{4}$ hours	$3\frac{1}{4}$ hours	$3\frac{3}{4}$ hours	$4\frac{1}{4}$ hours	$5\frac{1}{4}$ hours	6–$6\frac{1}{2}$ hours
Brandy	3 tblsp	4 tblsp	5 tblsp	5 tblsp	6 tblsp	7 tblsp	7 tblsp	2 tblsp

Sponge cake

Butter	100(4oz)	150g(6oz)	200g(8oz)	250g(10oz)	300g(12oz)	350g(14oz)	400g(16oz)	450g(18oz
Caster sugar	100g(4oz)	150g(6oz)	200g(8oz)	250g(10oz)	300g(12oz)	350g(14oz)	400g(16oz)	450g(18oz)
Medium eggs	2	3	4	5	6	7	8	9
SR flour	100g(4oz)	150g(6oz)	200g(8oz)	250g(10oz)	300g(12oz)	350g(14oz)	400g(16oz)	450g(18oz)
Ground rice	50g(2oz)	75g(3oz)	100g(4oz)	125g(5oz)	150g(6oz)	175g(7oz)	200g(8oz)	225g(9oz)
Grated lemon rind	$\frac{1}{2}$ lemon	1 lemon	$1\frac{1}{2}$ lemon	2 lemons	2 $\frac{1}{2}$ lemons	3 lemons	3 $\frac{1}{2}$ lemons	4 lemons
lemon juice	2 teasp	1 tblsp	4 teasp	2 tblsp	6 teasp	3 tblsp	8 teasp	4 tblsp
approx cooking time	1 hour	1 $\frac{1}{4}$ hours	1 hour 20 minutes	1 $\frac{1}{2}$ hours	1 $\frac{3}{4}$ hours	2 hours	2 $\frac{1}{4}$ hours	2 $\frac{1}{2}$ hours

OTHER CRAFT TITLES

DECORATING CAKES FOR CHILDREN'S PARTIES
by Polly Pinder

Thirty-one cakes tastefully illustrated in full colour plus 424 step-by-step drawings that will inspire the reader to make these stunning and delightful cakes. Cake ideas include Humpty Dumpty, Superman, Winnie-the-Pooh, Fast-food addict.

HOMEMADE and at a fraction of the cost
by Polly Pinder

'An imaginative and practical book full of ideas, recipes and instructions for making breads, chutneys, drinks, sweets, soft cheese, soaps. Superb colour photographs.' *The Lady.* Cased and paperback.

MADE TO TREASURE
Embroideries for all Occasions edited by Kit Pyman.

This book offers a rich variety of ideas for embroideries to be made to commemorate special occasions – christenings, weddings, birthdays – from simple greetings cards to a gold-work panel for a golden wedding. A heart warming present precisely because it is specially made.

THE SPLENDID SOFT TOY BOOK

The Splendid Soft Toy Book contains a wealth of ideas and pictures for making a wide variety of toys and dolls, from a green corduroy crocodile to detailed traditional, even collectors' dolls. More than 60 full colour pictures and over 70 black and white illustrations show the reader how to fashion appealing figures and animals of all shapes and sizes. Cased and paperback.

THE CHRISTMAS CRAFTS BOOK

Creative ideas and designs for the whole family to make objects with a Christmas flavour: table and room decorations, stars, Christmas tree ornaments, candles and candlesticks, angels, nativity scenes, paper chains and Christmas cards.

EVERY KIND OF PATCHWORK
edited by Kit Pyman

'Really lives up to its title, and is sufficiently easy to follow that even the most helpless needleperson would be tempted to have a go. But there's plenty, too, for the experienced.' *The Guardian.* Cased and Paperback.

EVERY KIND OF SMOCKING
edited by Kit Pyman

The description of the basic technique is followed by sections on children's clothes, fashion smocking, experimental smocking and creative ideas for finishing touches.

HOW TO MAKE BEAUTIFUL FLOWERS
edited by Valerie Jackson

How to make flowers from all sorts of materials; silk, paper, shells, bread dough, feathers, seeds. The instructions are simple, the materials inexpensive and easy to obtain.

If you are interested in any of the above books or any of the art and craft titles published by Search Press please send for free catalogue to: Search Press Ltd., Dept B, Wellwood, North Farm Road, Tunbridge Wells, Kent. TN2 3DR.